FROM
THE LIFE
OF THE
MARIONETTES

ALSO BY INGMAR BERGMAN

AUTUMN SONATA
THE SERPENT'S EGG
SCENES FROM A MARRIAGE
FACE TO FACE

FROM THE LIFE OF THE MARIONETTES

Ingmar Bergman

Translated from the Swedish by Alan Blair

PANTHEON BOOKS
New York

All rights reserved under International and Pan-American Copyright Conventions. Published in the United States by Pantheon Books, a division of Random House, Inc., New York, and simultaneously in Canada by Random House of Canada Limited, Toronto. Originally published in Sweden as *Ur Marionetternas Liv* by Norstedt & Soner Forlag. Copyright © 1979 by Ingmar Bergman.

Library of Congress Cataloging in Publication Data

Bergman, Ingmar, 1918–
    From the life of the marionettes.

    Translation of Ur marionetternas liv.
    I. Title.
PN1997.U53713 1980   839.7′274   80–7698
ISBN 0–394–51317–7
ISBN 0–394–73970–1 (pbk.)

The photographs throughout this book were taken by Arne Carlsson.

Manufactured in the United States of America

FIRST AMERICAN EDITION

Preface

Dear Collaborators!

In the first part of *Scenes from a Marriage* appear two furious and disastrous persons whom I called Peter and Katarina. They should really have been given much more room for their drama in *Scenes*, but Johan and Marianne took up all the space, and I had to remain silent about the further vicissitudes of the perilous couple. In a screenplay that was designed on a large scale and on the whole turned out to be a failure *(Love Without Lovers)*, Peter and Katarina's marital disaster occurs as one of several themes. The film foundered, but the two refused to go to the bottom with the rest of the wreckage. They kept stubbornly recurring in my plans. Scenes took shape, and now *From the Life of the Marionettes* is a fact.

The action takes place between different time levels (before and after the catastrophe); and, in addition, flashbacks are interspersed with the individual scenes. This sounds complicated and difficult to read but will no doubt be easy to understand in the completed film. For the sake of clarity, I have provided headings and proper indications of time; they will not be needed in the final product (I hope!).

From force of habit, in the preface to my screenplays

I try to show why I have written the film. It is not always so easy. Rationalization and sententiousness lie in wait. In this case, however, it is fairly simple: Why does a short-circuit reaction occur in a person who is in every way well adjusted and well established? *Face to Face* dealt with a similar theme, but here the person's actions are disastrous and involve someone else. How and why, therefore, does a short-circuit reaction occur?

In fairly short scenes, which are often broken off or deliberately torn to pieces, I try, as an outsider, to record the minutes, as it were. I have refrained from all interference, which means of course that objectivity is nevertheless a pure illusion. None of the performers, however, can claim to elucidate or clarify the drama. They are all implicated and thus perplexed. (The psychiatrist, who by reason of his profession should be nearest to understanding, is the farthest away.)

The intention is that those who want to or think it is exciting should draw their own conclusions; those who don't want to can, it is hoped, view it all as entertainment.

January 1980
Fårö

FROM
THE LIFE
OF THE
MARIONETTES

I—A Conversation on a High Level

MOGENS   I think the time was five o'clock or soon after. I had just gotten up and gone into the hall to get the paper—I am a very early riser—when the telephone rang. I remember being vexed with myself for having forgotten to disconnect the phone for the night—patients often call me up at all hours. At first I ignored the rings, but finally answered, not wanting my wife —who sleeps in the room next-door—to wake up.

It was Peter Egerman on the phone. He was quite calm, and his voice was fully under control. He asked me to come to a certain address. I was to go in through the street door, cross the backyard, and look for an iron door to the left of the staircase. He said he had found a key and would let me in.

I was there in about twenty minutes. The time was five thirty or just after. We went down some cellar steps and opened a door. The whole place was brightly lit, and a tape recorder was making a hideous noise. The girl was lying prostrate over a table in the fairly large dressing room. She was covered with a large brocade cloth and was naked from the waist down. Her legs had been spread wide apart. Her face was bloodstained, swollen, and discolored (for further details see the autopsy report). Peter Egerman said he

3

had murdered the girl and then had anal intercourse with her. He was still quite calm, almost indifferent. While I was phoning for ambulance and police, he sat on a chair in the corridor, smoking a cigarette.

INTERROGATOR   Professor Jensen—I'd be grateful if you would regard our talk entirely as an informal contact. Not only are you one of our most eminent psychiatric experts, but you have been a close friend of Mr. Egerman and his wife for many years.

MOGENS   Naturally I'm prepared to answer your questions as frankly as I can. But to tell the truth, I'm deeply shocked. I've known Peter Egerman for the last twenty years. A very talented, charming, conscientious man, liked by all. To the best of my knowledge, happily married to a clever professional woman. A large circle of friends. A comfortable, fairly quiet life. A delightful mother—

INTERROGATOR   Cordelia Egerman.

MOGENS   His father died some time ago. The family is well-off. Peter's brother is ambassador in Vienna. His sister is married to a prominent businessman.

INTERROGATOR   No hereditary tendency to depression or other disturbances?

MOGENS   Not as far as I know.

INTERROGATOR   Has either Peter or Katarina ever consulted you for any kind of trouble?

MOGENS   Nothing worse than what could be remedied by a little Valium or Mogadon.

II—Peter Goes to the Doctor

Flashback in black-and-white

(PROFESSOR MOGENS JENSEN's *private consulting room is bright and airy, well isolated from the outside world.* PETER EGERMAN *paces restlessly over the extensive carpet, perhaps stopping for a moment to look at one of the professor's exquisite Asiatic objets d'art or the splendid view over a wintry city. The doctor is standing with his back to the room, studying his notes. He has switched on the desk lamp)*

PETER   It was good of you to see me on a Saturday.

MOGENS   I always come here for a few hours on the weekend anyway.

PETER How long can you spare?

MOGENS An hour or so. I'm expecting a visitor.

PETER You'll let me know?

MOGENS I'll let you know.

PETER A patient?

MOGENS You don't smoke? Won't you sit down?

PETER Only when I drink. Does it bother you if I walk about?

MOGENS *(Sitting down)* Not in the least.

PETER I keep thinking: Next week it will be better. After all, I'm a living human being surrounded by other living human beings. Logically, I must change from one second to the next. So tomorrow I'll find a solution. Or maybe the day after tomorrow, or next

week. I have a recklessly positive attitude to actual living. Oh, I know it's cruel. Children starve, men tear each other's guts out and a friend's leukemia is not to be made light of, but I'm damned if it isn't beautiful on a clear autumn morning, and I enjoy good food, and success is a fine thing, and it's useful to earn money. Katarina is pretty, wonderfully intelligent, and very capable. We love each other. I'm not being ironical, please don't think I'm ironical—I have every reason to be sincere. It would certainly not be very wise to try on ambiguities or double meanings with you, especially as your time is limited. I've kept too many late hours recently and drunk a bit too much, and the days pass all right. Well. Now I'll tell you what brings me, without beating about the bush. I suppose everyone has something that makes them anxious. Don't you think? My worry is, I think, rather special. That's why I've come to you. You're wondering why I talk so much. It's true. I can't bring myself to tell you what's worrying me. So long as I don't utter the words, my anxiety is like a dream, unreal. When I've said the words, I'll have manifested my anxiety.

(MOGENS *is a tall man with a heavy, suntanned face, bushy hair, large nose, wide mouth with thick lips, and a low forehead. His eyes are blue with brown flecks; he is inclined to peer, and this gives his face an energetic expression)*

PETER It frightens me that I want to kill. It frightens me that I want to kill a human being. It frightens me. I want to kill my wife. I want to kill her. For two years I have lived with the thought of killing Katarina. Let me tell you of something strange that happened some years ago, at the beginning of our marriage: It was a hot summer's day, a Sunday. For some reason we were at home in the apartment. We had made love and slept nearly all day. Katarina came out of the bathroom, naked. I was lying on the bed. I stretched out my hand for her to come up to me. She smiled—

(PETER *breaks off and strokes his face with both hands. The fair, thin hair falls over his brow, the gold-rimmed spectacles are lying on the carpet, the delicate skin blushes above the narrow, high forehead. The boyish, forty-year-old* PETER EGERMAN *tries in vain to tell of the singular moment when he became aware for the first time that he wanted to kill his wife. The thin lips try out different words, which remain unsaid*)

PETER   I know what you're thinking. Prolonged erotic exercises and thoughts of death are a rather banal combination.

MOGENS   Never mind what I think.

PETER   Katarina has been unfaithful to me, and I've been unfaithful to her. That's beside the point. There's no glass wall between Katarina and me. *(Pause)* I called you up on Friday, didn't I? I had killed her then. I got up early in the morning and sat down at my desk to work. It was useless. I began at once to kill her. She came toward me smiling. She was naked; her thick hair was damp. It's the same every time. She is naked and comes toward me smiling. We have it good in bed, amazingly good really. We make love— how shall I put it?—with no feeling. I mean, without thinking of what we feel for each other. I'm not used to describing mental complications. I suspect you already know that, so I needn't say it. We like our pleasure or maybe each other's pleasure, I don't know exactly. It has been best when we've been unfaithful on both sides. I use the word "unfaithful," but it's wrong. It has a negative, moral ring about it. And we have never—"mutual sexual freedom," I think it's called. I do run on, don't I? You see how helpless I am.

(PETER *hunches his shoulders. He laughs resignedly and wipes his over-moist lips with the back of his hand*)

PETER   Psychiatrists are usually interested in dreams. My dreams are trivial, nondescript, and insipid. One afternoon—it was last Sunday, we were in the country with Katarina's parents—I dreamed that Katarina and I woke up in a sealed, shadowless room. We were naked and thirsty. *(Breaks off)* Strange to be—

MOGENS   *(After a pause)* To be what?

PETER   I can't remember.

MOGENS   *(After a long pause)* Well?

PETER   I want you to tell me that my fixed idea about Katarina's death is a matter of hormones. Maybe I want you to hypnotize me. That would be a solution! You don't say anything.

MOGENS   Let me tell you that you embarrass me. Just why did you come? You don't believe in your own torments.

PETER   I don't believe—

MOGENS   My dear Peter. People like you don't believe that the mind exists. So I don't understand your visit.

PETER   No. Hm, I see. No.

MOGENS   You have disturbed me for long enough.

PETER   Are you angry?

MOGENS   Of course I'm angry—you show such little respect for your own fear.

PETER   Well, you can give me a tranquilizer at any rate.

MOGENS   Why?

PETER   You want to pack me off, out into the snow and—

MOGENS   Go for a brisk walk. An excellent remedy for a fit of the blues and depressing thoughts. Then have some strong coffee and a couple of brandies. You'll feel like a new man.

PETER   *(After a long pause)* I don't want to.

MOGENS   Sit down.

PETER   I thought I really made an effort. *(Laughs)*

MOGENS   Not particularly.

PETER   Is it serious?

MOGENS   You mean about Katarina?

PETER   Yes.

MOGENS   It depends.

PETER   You're going to speak to Katarina.

MOGENS   I don't know. I think so.

PETER   My God.

MOGENS   Have you yourself—

PETER   *(Interrupting)* How often do we say that we hate? Or that we wish other people were dead? Or hit them? Or humiliate, defy, threaten them? We spit at each other, grip each other's arms, wrestle, shout. A little blood is shed, one triumphs, the other is contrite, stands at the bathroom door and apologizes. It's all quite harmless, isn't it?

MOGENS   Yes. Awfully harmless.

PETER   It's all like a play with the lines rehearsed, and pauses, outbursts, and exits all prepared. The lack of an audience of course is fatal, but that inconvenience can usually be rectified. *(Hides his face)*

MOGENS   *(After a pause)* All that—

PETER   All that is nothing. A familiar part of our married life, I think—no, that doesn't make sense either.

MOGENS   Doesn't make sense?

PETER   Isn't there an idiotic notion that some poor fools love their fights, their mutual humiliations? That it's supposed to be some exquisite form of contact? I get a bash on the nose—hurrah! we're touching each other! *(Laughs)* Divorce and all that!

MOGENS   How do you kill her?

PETER   You want me to describe how I kill her? I can't. I won't. It's only a fantasy. It's nothing but a nightmare that comes to me suddenly.

MOGENS   Fairly palpable.

PETER   Like herself.

(MOGENS   *is silent*)

PETER   It's she who wants to.

(MOGENS   *is silent*)

PETER   She wants me to kill her.

MOGENS   In your mind?

PETER   I don't know.

(MOGENS   *is silent*)

PETER   Maybe it's in my mind. Maybe it's real. I mean
that she—I don't know. How do you expect me to
know? We've never—

MOGENS   Never?

PETER   There's something—something about her lips.
(Stares at the doctor in mild surprise) I can't explain.

(MOGENS   *is silent, looks at*   PETER)

PETER   Does it worry you if you can't elucidate a process? He wants to fuck his mother and she in her turn
has been all muddled up in relation to her father and
so she wants to be— How can you stand all that?

MOGENS No one is cured with explanations.

PETER *Is* there a cure?

MOGENS Yes, for a broken leg and appendicitis and one or two other things.

PETER But the much-discussed mind?

MOGENS I don't think so.

PETER Doesn't it drive you to despair?

MOGENS I'm not the despairing kind.

PETER If you don't believe in a cure, why do you go on?

MOGENS Out of curiosity.

PETER Is there a way out?

MOGENS In another society there might be ways out.

PETER So you're all for another society?

MOGENS No.

PETER What do you believe in?

MOGENS Does it interest you?

PETER Quite a lot, actually.

MOGENS Right inside the utter madness there is kindness, unselfishness, tenderness, and art. It is quite inexplicable and for that very reason—how shall I put it?—edifying. There is an almost unexplored power, which we call self-healing. It astonishes us constantly and frustrates our prognoses.

PETER Is that self-healing everywhere?

MOGENS Of course. But we obstruct it.

PETER   *(Very upset)* Obstruct! It's not true. I exert myself, I don't obstruct. The days pass, the hours, the
minutes. The anxiety, the fantasies, the compulsion.
I'm not afraid of death. Yes, I am. I'm horribly afraid,
Mogens! Death is literally standing behind my back
with his hand on my shoulder. Does it sound absurd?
I can smell decay. All that is allowed for in my plans
for Katarina's death. Perhaps after all a release. No,
that's not true either. Why do we never touch bottom,
Mogens? Is there no decisive truth? *(Laughs)* I've a
genius for finding the right words, haven't I? *(Laughs)*
Death follows me everywhere; maybe it's he who pulls
the strings and makes me laugh. *I shall kill Katarina,
I've said so, you're the witness.* Then I'll kill myself—it's
thought out and goes without saying. It's what you
call "extended suicide," isn't it? As I'm so afraid of
death, I want to die myself; but poor Katarina is to
give it concrete form and make it irrevocable. *(Pause)*
It's not as easy as that.

MOGENS   No, it's not as easy as that.

PETER   There's bright sunlight and not a sound in the
apartment. We've been left to ourselves for several
days, maybe even longer. We haven't quarreled, all is
still, perhaps it's early morning. The street is quiet
and empty. The sunlight dazzles me as I draw back the
thick curtain—the whole bedroom seems to quiver
with light. I sit on the bed and lean back against the
pillows with a feeling of peace. Everything is fairly
remote—I mean work, everyday life, voices, and
agreements. No excitement or worry. The bathroom
door is open. I can see her moving about in there,
bathed in the strong, almost unreal sunlight. She is
naked and is combing her long hair, looking at herself
in the mirror. I've always enjoyed watching my wife.

Even when we have hated each other or she has been repulsive, tipsy, ill, or merely spiteful. I have always delighted in her movements, her smell, her presence. There's something about her . . . Most people's bodies are dead with talking heads and flapping extremities. Katarina is so . . . She stands there, combing her hair, turning now this way, now the other. There is a stillness around us, as though of expectation. She turns toward me and looks at me and there is something about her lips, she opens her lips . . . Has it ever struck you that her lips have a most unusual shape? She looks at me without seeing me, she often does. Formerly, when we were in love, I used to see red. Now it fascinates me. She doesn't see me, I don't think she's even aware of my presence. I like her indifference, it gets me excited. Not now, now it's something else, a complete silence, a complete— I am standing behind her, not close, there must be a couple of feet between us. She is turned toward the big mirror that covers the whole wall to the right of the window. The panes are of frosted glass and the light sparkles, hurting my eyes. She sees me in the mirror, but she doesn't see me. She is deep in thought but is breathing heavily. I am standing behind her, obliquely behind her. We are both naked, and I am holding the open razor in my left hand. She strokes her thick, glossy hair with her left hand, puts down the heavy comb, bends her right arm, and lays the palm of her hand against her temple. Then she takes a small step backward, quite a small step, very slowly and precisely, like all her movements. She never takes her eyes off me, *and now she really sees me* and forms her lips into a faint smile. I can feel her light touch, her skin against my skin. Her shoulders are gleaming, still damp from the bath, her hair is fragrant, and a tiny pulse is throbbing at her neck.

MOGENS   Do you realize that a human being contains an amazing amount of blood? If you cut the carotid artery, blood spurts on the walls and you yourself will be covered with it. Blood is sticky and has a fairly strong smell. Moreover, your victim doesn't die immediately —it takes several minutes before she loses consciousness. Presumably, both you and she have time to think quite a lot. Perhaps you begin to feel sick and suddenly you have to vomit. How is it to be? Shall you take your own life in the same way? Maybe you're sorry. It didn't turn out the way you thought. It wasn't the wonderful, supernatural experience you had hoped. It was all different somehow, except that Katarina is lying on the bath mat with a gash in her throat from which the blood is bubbling and pulsating.

PETER   You're being sarcastic, aren't you?

MOGENS   No. I am almost convinced that you intend to commit some act which in your imagination will reveal you in reality or in a special kind of reality that exists only in your dreams. I don't know. If you like, I'll arrange for you to be admitted to my clinic. There we'll give you every known injection so that at last you won't give a damn whether you're Peter Egerman or the emperor of China. Don't worry, we're phenomenal at obliterating people's identities. No self, no fear. Fantastic, isn't it?

PETER   I don't know.

MOGENS   You're a proper little bureaucrat. Your first thought is that you'll be neglecting your work. It's right, Peter. You see your fine desk in front of you, with papers that have to be read and commented on; you see your diary with all the appointments and lunches. Which is it to be?

PETER *(Smiling wanly)* I read somewhere that the latest mind cure is so delightfully tough.

MOGENS I'm saying that I take you seriously.

PETER I'm extremely grateful.

MOGENS You're so well behaved, well adjusted, well groomed, well educated, well prospered. I've always thought you suspiciously perfect.

PETER I'm detaining you.

MOGENS A trifle. To tell the truth, I'm expecting a visitor.

PETER Then I won't disturb you any longer.

MOGENS If you come back on Thursday at four o'clock, we can sit and talk for an hour or two. I'll have no patients waiting then.

PETER Nice of you.

MOGENS Yes, isn't it.

PETER Shall I tell Katarina that I—

MOGENS I'll phone her.

PETER That's better.

MOGENS I want to ask her one or two things.

PETER I see.

MOGENS Good-bye, Peter Egerman. Take care of yourself.

PETER Good-bye, Mogens. Have a nice time.

MOGENS What do you mean?

PETER Your visitor.

MOGENS   You know your way?

PETER   Of course.

(PETER   *passes a short corridor leading to a handsomely
furnished waiting room. He stops at the hall door, opens it,
and shuts it again. Then he pushes open a door to the long hall.
The wide doors are ajar and he can see into the waiting room,
where the professor is visible, as if on a brightly lighted stage.
The elevator machinery hums faintly, and piano music can
be heard somewhere; otherwise it is very quiet. The professor
lights a cigarette, stands for a few moments by one of the big
windows, then goes over to the desk, dials a number, waits for
some time, puts the phone down with an impatient gesture,
then dials another number and gets an immediate reply)*

MOGENS   Mrs. Egerman? May I speak to Mrs. Egerman,
please? It's urgent, yes, it's urgent. Professor Jensen.
I beg your pardon? Yes, that's better. I'll wait.

*(He stubs out the cigarette, sits in the desk chair, but gets up
at once)*

MOGENS   Katarina? Peter has been here; he has just gone.
Can you come? You'll come straightaway? I'll put the
door on the latch.

(MOGENS   *puts the phone down, takes off his glasses, tidies
the papers on his desk, passes the dark hall, puts the hall
door on the latch, goes into the toilet, switches on the light,
washes his hands and dries them on a paper towel, which he
throws into a small basket, puts the light out, goes out on to
the landing, and listens for sounds from below. The piano
music is a little louder. He digs his hands into his trouser
pockets, regards his well-polished shoes, whistles to himself,
and returns to the hall. He is now standing quite close to
PETER.   He looks at himself in a large mirror, pulls off his
tie and opens his shirt collar, takes off his coat, disap-*

pears from sight, returns wearing a sporty cardigan, sits down at his desk, puts on his glasses, and begins to write something in a large notebook with green covers.

The elevator whines, the grille door rattles, there are quick footsteps, the hall door opens and shuts. PETER *can see her. She has no hat or makeup, snowflakes are still melting on her shoulders, and her cheeks are rosy with the cold. She is wearing black slacks, a black jumper with a high collar, and high-heeled boots. She throws off a short suède coat that has a masculine cut. The doctor stands up and goes toward her. They embrace and he kisses her on both cheeks, quite near the corners of her mouth)*

KATARINA   Sorry to be so long, I had to park the car some distance away so as not to . . . I ran the last bit, it's turned so damn cold. How are you? Let me see you. You look flourishing. Have you anything to drink?

MOGENS   How's the fashion show?

KATARINA   Shaping up pretty well. Are you coming?

MOGENS   Fanny will be there. I haven't time. I'm to give a lecture at the Medical Society and must stay at home and prepare it.

KATARINA   Then you're off to Tunisia.

MOGENS   On Friday.

KATARINA   And will be away—?

MOGENS   For six weeks.

KATARINA   Alone?

MOGENS   Of course.

KATARINA   What a delicious wine. And your wife?

MOGENS For the last seven years we've taken our vacations at different times.

KATARINA Oh yes, you told me.

MOGENS Come with me.

KATARINA To Tunisia?

MOGENS Why not?

KATARINA And Peter?

MOGENS He might think it would be practical.

KATARINA *(After a short pause)* You with all your cleverness—can't you see I love my husband?

MOGENS Have you never been—

KATARINA Often, far too often. But that's different.

MOGENS I don't follow.

KATARINA You don't have to.

MOGENS But my curiosity is whetted.

KATARINA I think you're attractive, I even think we'd thoroughly enjoy a fuck. Going away is another matter entirely. Eating together, waking up and going to sleep together—no, thank you. Thanks for the offer, but I'll stay with Peter. He's insufferable, but he's mine.

MOGENS If you should change your mind, you can let me know.

KATARINA I won't promise.

(They are outlined sharply against the white window curtains. They stand facing each other, and the doctor's broad, pale hand is resting on her hip)

MOGENS   And now?

KATARINA   I didn't come here to have it off with you but to talk about Peter. Anyway, I'm having my period.

MOGENS   Two miserable pretexts.

KATARINA   We can't stay here at any rate.

MOGENS   No, we can't stay here.

KATARINA   Have you any suggestions?

MOGENS   In there. *(Points to the consulting room)*

KATARINA   Not the first time, eh?

MOGENS   No, as a matter of fact.

KATARINA   Where's the bathroom?

   (MOGENS   *takes her by the hand, leads her through the hall, opens the door to the narrow corridor, opens another door)*

MOGENS   There you are.

(KATARINA *closes the door.* MOGENS *stands for a few moments with his head bent and a smile on his lips. Then he goes into the consulting room and begins to undress.* KATARINA *can be heard moving about, singing to herself. There is a roaring in the pipes, then a sudden silence.* MOGENS *becomes aware of it and stops undressing. The bathroom door opens slowly and* KATARINA *comes out, pulling the black jumper over her head. She is fully dressed except that her feet are bare)*

KATARINA   I'm sorry, but I can't.

MOGENS   Can't. *(Smiles gently)*

KATARINA   I really do think it would be nice, but I can't.

MOGENS   Is it Peter?

KATARINA   Yes, it's Peter.

MOGENS   How touching.

KATARINA   Why are you being sarcastic?

MOGENS   I'm not. Word of honor.

(Avoiding his eyes and his smile, KATARINA *makes a deprecating gesture and returns to the waiting room. The daylight is fading and has turned gray and bleak)*

MOGENS   Peter wanted to talk to me.

KATARINA   *(Impatient)* That's why I'm here.

MOGENS   He makes out he is tormented by a certain definite obsession.

KATARINA   An obsession?

MOGENS   A fixed idea.

KATARINA   Is it serious?

MOGENS   Many people exaggerate the importance of their anxieties. They grow afraid, and the fear is actually worse than the idea itself.

KATARINA   And the idea?

MOGENS   Morbid fantasies of death. Thoughts of suicide. Murder, assault, violence. I don't quite know what. He's coming back on Thursday and we'll begin to sort it all out.

KATARINA   Is there any risk of his—

MOGENS   It's not very likely.

KATARINA   Why don't you send him to the hospital?

MOGENS   He doesn't want to go.

KATARINA   What if he harms himself?

MOGENS   In that case I can admit him.

KATARINA   So something has to happen first?

MOGENS   More or less.

KATARINA   What am *I* to do?

MOGENS   Perhaps you should go away for a while.

KATARINA   In the middle of the season! What a suggestion. Besides, why should I go away? If Peter's ill, he needs someone to look after him.

MOGENS   There's a slight but distinct possibility that you yourself might come to harm.

KATARINA   What do you mean? Would Peter—

MOGENS   Yes.

KATARINA   Has he said that—

MOGENS   He hinted at it.

KATARINA   It seems utterly absurd.

MOGENS   So you can't go away?

KATARINA   Quite out of the question. You must see that.

MOGENS   Could you have someone to stay, a temporary guest?

KATARINA   Peter would never hear of it.

MOGENS   Haven't you two nephews?

KATARINA   Boys of six and eight in the house? Impossible.

MOGENS   Can *Peter* go away for a time?

KATARINA   He's madly busy. They're in the middle of awfully complicated negotiations.

MOGENS   I'll put him on the sick list for a month or two.

KATARINA   I'm afraid that's quite unrealistic.

MOGENS   Then for the moment I can think of nothing else.

KATARINA   I'm wondering if, deep down, you're not more worried than you'll admit.

MOGENS   Common sense tells me the risks are infinitesimal.

KATARINA   Let's stick to common sense then.

MOGENS   I don't know, Katarina. My intuition is damnably disturbed.

KATARINA   Is your intuition always right?

MOGENS   I think so.

KATARINA   I, too, have intuition.

MOGENS   And what does it tell you?

KATARINA   It tells me that, consciously or unconsciously, you're trying to get at the relationship between me and Peter.

MOGENS   Any reason?

KATARINA   I don't know. Perhaps you're that sort of person.

MOGENS   *(Gives a laugh, then is serious)* Well, I'm damned.

KATARINA   I've always been a little afraid of you.

MOGENS   Not *only* afraid?

KATARINA   Peter is a part of me, don't you see? I carry him with me wherever I go; he's here inside me. I've never felt like that about anyone else. If we'd had children, maybe it would be different—now we're each other's child. No, that's not true. Neither of us wants to grow up. That's why we fight and quarrel and cry our eyes out. Neither of us wants to be wise and mature. But we have the same circulation, our nerve centers have grown together in some awful way. Can you understand that? Peter's in pain, so at once I get a pain. Peter and everyone else say that I am so damned strong. Outwardly that's true. I'm capable and conscientious and intelligent, or so everyone says —a sort of female paragon. Then Peter gets ill and I'm supposed to cope, but I get ill myself. I can't help him with anything, and he can't help me. I keep shivering. I want to rush home to Peter and hold him tight and say: From now on I understand everything you say, everything you think, everything you feel. I want to hold him tight until he is aware of me. What the hell is it that stops us from seeing each other, although we live close together and know everything about each other? Now I'll have a cigarette and calm down.

MOGENS   Would you like another glass of wine?

KATARINA   No, you can keep your wine.

MOGENS   You needn't be rude to me just because you're worried about Peter.

KATARINA   I like being unfair to you. It's good for you.

MOGENS   I've a suggestion.

KATARINA   Well?

MOGENS   Let's combat our misery, sorrow, and heaviness of heart. Let's defy the cold, the unseen powers, the fading light, and the tedium and go for a brisk walk in the park.

KATARINA   That's the last straw!

MOGENS   Come along, Katarina.

KATARINA   And what shall we talk about?

MOGENS   Food, for instance. Or flowers.

KATARINA   You're awfully tired of me. Be honest now.

MOGENS   No, I'm certainly not tired of you.

(KATARINA *and* MOGENS *chatter gaily to each other as they put on their coats and leave the apartment.* PETER *steps out from his hiding place. Suddenly he gives a start. Inside an alcove he catches a glimpse of a crouching figure with a face like a white blob, vacant eye sockets, tight lips, and hanging arms. It takes him nearly two seconds to recognize his own reflection. He opens his mouth and lets out a soft moan. It sounds inhuman)*

III—Conversation with Peter Egerman's Mother

INTERROGATOR   I'd be grateful if you would tell me something about your son.

MRS. EGERMAN   It's hard. It's all so hard to understand. *(Pause)* He was always so kind and thoughtful. He used to call up every day and we'd have a heart-to-heart talk. *(Pause)* We were never at odds. Not of recent years. I remember only one terrible quarrel. A terrible quarrel and a terrible outburst. I mean that Peter had a terrible outburst. But that was long ago. His father was seriously ill; he had had surgery for a tumor in the throat and had got double pneumonia. I phoned Peter and asked him to go and see his father. He refused. I was appalled, and naturally wondered why he wouldn't go to see his dying father. He said he had never had any emotional ties to his father, that he had always disliked him and couldn't care less about him. I had never heard him speak in that way and was of course very upset. I begged him to think twice about it and said he would regret it. He lost his temper and shouted at me to leave him alone, calling me a hypocrite as I myself detested my husband. I told Peter it wasn't true, that I loved and respected his father, that we had lived together for forty years and the least he could do was to go and see him for my sake. Then he shouted at me that he wouldn't stand for emotional blackmail and that I was to stop always trying to force him. I was speechless, as I had never before heard such words from my son. That same evening he did visit his father and sat with him for several hours. Later that night we met in the hospital corridor. Peter embraced me and kissed me and said he was sorry. He explained that he hadn't slept for several days, that he'd had a row with Katarina—they quarrel quite a lot, it's not a good marriage. I admire and respect Peter's wife, but it's not a good marriage, she is far too domineering. I don't think Katarina is too happy either. Of course we never discuss such things. Katarina and I get on very well together, we've no fault to find in each other. But we're not in close touch, much to my regret. Katarina has changed a lot too during the last few years. After her miscarriage (if it *was* a miscarriage, I'm not so sure) she devoted most of her time to her career. She is very successful and uncommonly talented. I respect and admire her, but with the best will in the world I cannot see that she is the right wife for Peter. I suppose this is irrelevant to the matter in hand?

INTERROGATOR   I am grateful for all information.

MRS. EGERMAN   I think Peter exaggerated the aggression toward his father. My husband took part with affection and great interest in the children's upbringing. He tried never to dominate them or force them. On the contrary, he spurred them to independent thinking. Peter and his father were always on good terms. They were both fond of hunting and fishing and made long trips together. I don't know if they had any deeper contact, I don't know that of course, but my husband always spoke of Peter with pride and affection. *(Pause)* I am so helpless. What is it you want to know? *(Pause)* Peter was a longed-for child, we were so happy. He had a harmonious childhood. Too sheltered perhaps, I don't know. He was rather timid and afraid of the dark, he always wanted the light to be left burning outside the nursery. He was afraid of all sorts of things—dogs, horses, big birds.

His brothers and sisters were more robust. Peter took after me. I, too, was sensitive as a child and rather delicate—suffered from asthma and sudden allergies. I remember he bit his nails, it looked horrid. He was very attached to his younger sister; they played with dolls and had a puppet theater. He did well at school, always got top marks and had a much better head for study than his brothers and sisters. Peter's elder brother had a violent temper. His puberty was difficult. We had to send him to boarding school. Peter's adolescence, on the other hand, was quite harmonious. When he was twenty he met a very nice girl. They got engaged and were going to marry when they had finished studying. Then he met Katarina and fell head over heels in love. From the outset Katarina had great influence over him. It was she who decided everything. What Peter's parents thought didn't matter any more. *(Pause)* It's the way of the world, I suppose. *(Pause)* I don't know, it's beyond me. How can I be expected to understand? Before I married I was an actress, then I devoted myself to the children. My husband didn't want me to go on with my profession, and I have never regretted it. I've had a good and happy life. A few days ago Peter came on a hasty visit. He had just received a list of necessary repairs to the house. We went through it together, he was going to speak to the architect and the builders. It's a dilapidated old house, and the park has been neglected. In one wing the roof is so badly insulated that the damp comes in when the snow melts. We talked about all that. We were both in rather a hurry. I was expecting guests to dinner, and Peter was off to some conference. I noticed nothing unusual. He merely said he was rather tired and was getting over a cold. Katarina was in Paris but was coming back in the middle of the week. We laughed at all the repairs and at the architect's report; it was quite funny. Peter said I lived in a ruin. But I love my old house and will never leave it.

IV—Dead of Night

Flashback in black-and-white

KATARINA   Can't you sleep?

PETER   No.

KATARINA   Have you taken your Nembutal?

PETER   I've taken two.

KATARINA   You shouldn't drink so much.

PETER   No.

(It is night. The outlines of the window are seen against the reflected glow from the city. The heavy traffic on the motorway has not yet begun. It is the small hours and very quiet. PETER's *breath is labored)*

KATARINA   If you want to put the light on and read, I don't mind. I'll sleep anyway.

PETER   I think I'll get up for a while.

KATARINA   Shall I heat some milk?

PETER   No, thanks.

(PETER *sits up and swings his legs over the edge of the bed.* KATARINA *can see his bent back and projecting head; his face is a pale blur)*

KATARINA I think it's turning very cold. Shall I switch on the heating?

PETER Not for me.

(He rubs his face, straightens his back, and bends his head backward, swallowing repeatedly)

KATARINA How's the cold?

PETER Better, I think. My throat's not so sore.

KATARINA Oh, good.

(There is a long silence; neither of them moves. KATARINA *is falling asleep. Her breathing is light and even.* PETER *slowly turns his head. He can see her now almost clearly: the pale, high forehead; the thick hair plaited for the night; the childish mouth; the arched eyebrows; the stubborn, strong, discontented face.* PETER *shivers suddenly. He leans back against the piled-up pillows, wraps himself in the quilt, fumbles for the earphones, and presses a button on the little radio beside the bed. Booming electronic pop music fills his head. He endures it for a few moments, then switches off and hangs the earphones on the bedpost. He gets up, goes into the bathroom, catches sight of his swollen, pasty face, blotchy with sleeping pills, hunts among the pillboxes, finds what he is looking for, swallows, and gulps down some water out of the toothbrush glass. Then, wrapping himself in his shabby bathrobe, he shuffles out into the living room. He stands by the window, looking at the city spread out beyond the park—the brightly lighted office blocks where the cleaners have already begun their night's work, the floodlit churches, the red lights of the airport, the factory chimneys with their plumes of smoke, roofs beyond roofs, the leaden winter sky, heavy with snow*

—it is all familiar, yet now, in the dead of night, menacing and unreal. He looks in the cocktail cabinet and finds a half-empty bottle, fills a glass, hesitates for a moment, takes several sips, and screws up his face. His confounded stomach sends up warning signals, short aching protests. He glances at his left hand, which is shaking slightly; his wedding ring— his father's wedding ring—gleams. He puts a record on the turntable—Jean-Pierre Rampal's solo flute—and sinks down on the wide sofa. He pokes some cushions behind his back and tucks a rough yellow rug around him. He closes his eyes)

KATARINA   I can't sleep either.

PETER   It must be the change in the weather or the full moon or that damn disgusting dinner Oscar insisted on cooking himself.

KATARINA   What are you drinking?

PETER   *(Yawning)* Brandy.

KATARINA   I'll have something too.

PETER   Your horrible liqueur is there on the left.

KATARINA   Are you crazy, liqueur at three in the morning! I think I'll have a whiskey. It's both soothing and good for you.

PETER   You shouldn't drink so much either.

KATARINA   I'll drink as much as I like, my darling. Besides, I never lose control.

PETER   That's what *you* think.

KATARINA   If you've any faults to find, go ahead.

PETER   Do you realize how insufferable you were last night?

KATARINA I do, actually.

PETER It was because you drank too much.

KATARINA I did so on purpose.

PETER Oh, did you? On purpose!

KATARINA I like to embarrass Martin.

PETER You certainly succeeded.

KATARINA He will keep pawing me. So I tank up and paw back. Openly. It's a subtle way of getting even, don't you see, my sweet?

PETER You get shrill and giggly. *That* is not on purpose, surely.

KATARINA *You* think I get shrill and giggly. Everyone else thinks I'm amusing.

PETER   To hell with all dinner parties.

KATARINA   We have five next week.

PETER   You like them.

KATARINA   So do you.

PETER   I used to. Not any more.

KATARINA   Then there's your mother's lunch tomorrow.

PETER   It's important.

KATARINA   For you. Not for me.

PETER   It's a business matter.

KATARINA   I haven't time.

PETER   You promised.

KATARINA   Your business cronies think it an honor to
have a bad lunch with your awful old mother in that
dreadful ramshackle house. It's beyond me.

PETER   Mama is a monument.

KATARINA   A decaying monument to your father's goddamn tyranny.

PETER   (Laughs) Not that old song, Katarina.

KATARINA   (Draining her glass) Well, Katarina's off to bed.
I have to get up at a quarter to seven.

PETER   I'll sleep in the study.

KATARINA   Aren't you playing tennis?

PETER   Harry has a stiff arm.

KATARINA   He smokes too much.

PETER   Smoking doesn't give him a stiff arm.

KATARINA How do you know?

PETER I give up. His arm is hurting because—

KATARINA If you smoke sixty to seventy cigarettes a day, your circulation and muscles must be the worse for it.

PETER Yes, yes, of course. It affects the circulation.

KATARINA It goes without saying.

PETER It goes without saying that it goes without saying.

KATARINA So you don't want me to wake you when I go?

PETER When are you going?

KATARINA Just before eight.

PETER Wake me just before eight.

KATARINA Good night, my darling.

PETER Good night, my sweet.

(KATARINA *stands in the doorway to the little passage leading to the bedroom and bathroom. Her hand is resting against the doorpost. She can be dimly seen in the half-light from the softly shaded lamp by the sofa. She looks at her hand, at her arm, and then at* PETER)

KATARINA Peter.

PETER Yes.

KATARINA What is it that's wrong?

PETER Wrong? Everything's splendid as far as I know.

KATARINA No, it's wrong.

PETER   Always when you have your period we have to analyze what's wrong. Go to bed.

KATARINA   You can at least tell me why you're so terribly unhappy.

PETER   I'm neither unhappy nor happy. Damn awful word, come to think of it.

KATARINA   Have you worries?

PETER   On the contrary. Business has never been better, if that's what you mean.

KATARINA   *(Sadly)* No, that's not what I mean.

PETER   *(Kindly)* Thanks for your concern.

KATARINA   I don't understand that sort of heroism.

(She detaches herself from the half-light over by the door and goes and sits with him on the sofa, but at a distance and without looking at him. She runs her finger along the pattern of the fabric)

PETER   *(Kindly)* I'm looking for a way out. But all ways out are closed. If you know what I mean.

KATARINA   No.

PETER   No.

KATARINA   You must give me an example.

PETER   Ennui.

KATARINA   Ennui. I don't even know what it is.

PETER   *(With a laugh)* No, exactly!

KATARINA   I understand what the word means, but it tells me nothing. So you feel ennui.

PETER *(Smiling)* I feel ennui, yes. And a typical compo-
nent of ennui is that you feel an insurmountable ennui
in explaining how ennui works.

KATARINA *(After a short pause)* I wasn't going to tell you
this, but I will. No, it's nothing remarkable, just a
feeling. It was yesterday. Early in the morning. I was
in the bathroom, washing myself. I was rubbing my
skin with the towel, which was rough and newly
washed and smelled nice. Suddenly I had an . . . an
insight, for want of a better word. I looked at all these
familiar surroundings and knew that they would not
belong to me any more. Everything would be taken
from me. Nothing of what I saw, *nothing,* would be
mine. After a minute or two I'd forgotten all about it.
The feeling was gone nearly all day, but last evening
it came back several times. I thought the dinner party
was ghostly, unreal. My dress was not my dress, my
jewels were not mine. And when we got home—it was
no longer our home.

PETER *(In a whisper)* I'm tired, Katarina.

KATARINA Do you think you can sleep now?

PETER I took another Nembutal.

KATARINA Let's go to bed.

PETER What's the time?

KATARINA Nearly four.

PETER You can hear the long-distance trucks on the
motorway now.

V—Interlude

The following:
Béla Bartók—music for strings, percussion, and
celesta.
Third movement, *Adagio.*

(PETER   *is busy with a game of chess, which he is playing
against a small computer set at a high degree of difficulty. The
game slowly moves toward checkmate for the computer. Three
moves before the end, it gives up and a red light shows. The
room is small and spartanly furnished, the walls are bare and
painted green. In the door is a spy-hole. The windowpanes are
small and square. The ceiling light is on. The winter sun is
red on the horizon; a gray-blue haze hangs over the city to the
north. The columns of smoke from the factory chimneys rise
straight up toward the colorless evening sky. It is very cold.
The silence is complete. This is intended as a cinematographic
poem lasting six and a half minutes. It contains chiefly the
above elements, but* PETER's *face, mouth, hands, and posture
are the most important components. In addition, the setting
sun, the haze over the outlines of the city, the snowflakes, the
relentless traffic, the people in the darkening streets—all
soundless. When the music stops, a voice quietly comments on*
PETER's   *state)*

NURSE   *(Voice)* As soon as he has got up, had breakfast,
and made his bed (he gets up before all the others), he
sits down to his game of chess. He sets the computer
at a high degree of difficulty and sometimes lets the
game go on for several days. He is very polite to the
staff but at the same time standoffish. He won't have
any visitors, neither his wife nor his mother. He is
very particular about his hygiene, and he tidies his
room at least once a day. He is fussy about the bed-
spread—it takes him nearly a quarter of an hour to get

it as smooth and neat as he wants. He doesn't read any books or newspapers, he doesn't listen to the radio or watch TV. Sometimes he gets a bad fit of depression but he won't ask for help, rebuffing all our attempts at contact. At nights he has a worn-out old teddy bear beside him in bed. Presumably a childhood memory.

VI—Katarina and Tim

Flashback in black-and-white

(Far inside the largest lounge of the newly built hotel, preparations are going on for the following day's fashion show. On a rostrum extending right across the room the models are being rehearsed by a friendly, soft-spoken choreographer. A pianist plays the same tune over and over. Men and women of uncertain extraction are in a state of feverish but controlled excitement. Apparently it is to be a show of summer dresses, swimsuits, and the like. Spotlights are tried out. Chairs are arranged. A brightly colored nonfigurative tapestry is hung on one of the dark, gleaming walls. Outside the big windows the winter day is brooding; the snow falls without a letup. In this organized chaos KATARINA *is ensconced in an armchair with her feet on a low table. She is busy with India-ink pen and block, sketching and explaining to an aging and rather indeterminate youth in colored glasses and with dyed hair.* PETER *approaches slowly)*

KATARINA   *That's* how it should be, not like *that.* You'll change it by tomorrow, won't you, Tim darling?

TIM No trouble at all, Katarina. Have you phoned Milan?

KATARINA I'll phone Ariadna this afternoon. She's the only one who can say what has become of everything. There was a strike all last week, but Bettina promised to send a consignment with a Danish charter plane, which should have come yesterday but was delayed by the blizzard. Have you spoken to Paul?

TIM I spoke to Paul ten minutes ago. He has been at the airport customs since eight o'clock this morning. He hasn't seen a sign of any plane and no one knows a thing.

KATARINA Anyway, we send no money. *(Catches sight of Peter)* Heavens, is it so late? I'll be right with you. Have you been waiting long? Everything here's in a muddle. A quarter of the collection hasn't arrived. What do you say to that? Bye-bye, darling.

(She gets up quickly, kisses TIM *good-bye, and gathers up her belongings.* PETER *helps her on with the warm, lightweight fur coat. She waves to the girls, the choreographer, the pianist, a woman journalist, a photographer, and several other persons of importance. They hurry out to the elevator, which fortunately has just appeared. A young woman with a robust and determined look comes out dragging a large, specially constructed traveling trunk. Behind it, one of the hotel porters can be glimpsed)*

KATARINA Oh, here you are. Is this the lot?

SECRETARY Paul's bringing the rest in a moment. Customs feels like working today. Hello, Peter. Are you leaving?

KATARINA We have to go to an idiotic lunch with Peter's mother. We're terribly late. I'll be back the minute I can get away.

(The automatic elevator doors have impatiently pushed the hotel porter in the back. They are now on their way down)

KATARINA   I must have a drink.

PETER   We're late already.

KATARINA   I must have a drink.

PETER   You'll get one there.

KATARINA   I must have something strong so that I can endure your mother and all those people. Please, Peter darling. We'll dash into the bar, it will take only two minutes.

(PETER   gives up, shrugs, and checks his impulse to look at the time)

PETER   I've read somewhere that a lack of punctuality is a sign of suppressed aggressiveness.

KATARINA   It's not suppressed with me.

PETER   No, but with me.

KATARINA   You're a punctuality neurotic.

PETER   For that very reason.

KATARINA   I don't get it.

PETER   Never mind.

(They hurry through the large lobby, find the bar, which at this hour is fairly full.   KATARINA   beckons to someone she knows, sees to it that she is served at once, and gulps down her drink)

KATARINA   I simply must have another. The same again, please Jack. *(To Peter)* Now you're madly annoyed.

PETER   Now I'm madly annoyed.

KATARINA It improves your looks. Your eyes go dark and you have color in your cheeks. I like you when you're—

PETER I'm merely tired.

KATARINA It was you who said we'd go to that lunch.

PETER I asked you first.

KATARINA You asked me after you'd already accepted.

PETER You know as well as I do that it's an important—

KATARINA Oh yes, the fate of the country is at stake.

PETER If only I knew why you must provoke me.

KATARINA I don't care how angry you get, but I simply must have another drink.

PETER Okay. I'll leave you and tell Mama you hadn't time.

KATARINA An excellent idea.

(PETER *leaves her in anger. Their bickering has been noticed in the rather cramped and crowded room.* KATARINA *laughs loudly for no reason and orders a drink from her friend* JACK, *who winks conspiratorially. She takes her glass and settles down in a cozy corner, which has just been vacated by a swarthy lounge-lizard and his deathly pale female companion.* KATARINA *closes her eyes, takes a deep breath, lights a cigarette, and smokes it slowly and with enjoyment.* TIM *appears and joins* KATARINA)

TIM Didn't you go to Peter's mother's luncheon party?

KATARINA No, just fancy.

TIM   Did you lose your tempers?

KATARINA   Peter did.

TIM   May I sit down?

KATARINA   How's it going up there?

TIM   Everything's under control. We've broken until four o'clock. I hope you don't mind.

KATARINA   What would I do without you?

TIM   What would *I* do without *you?*

KATARINA   Tim, darling, you're crazy.

TIM   Have you eaten?

KATARINA   I don't think so.

TIM   I've a bright idea. Come home with me for a couple of hours. You can have a rest, and I'll make a delicious salad.

KATARINA   I'm quite comfy here.

TIM   Come on now, Katarina. You need to get away for a while, and this is like a railway station.

KATARINA   I've a bad conscience.

TIM   Over Peter?

KATARINA   Yes, isn't it silly?

TIM   Come along, Katarina.

(KATARINA   *nods gravely. The big, energetic girl is suddenly shrunken and pale.*   TIM   *takes her by the hand and pilots her skillfully through the crowded bar. She is not quite sober.*   TIM's   *apartment is bursting with knickknacks)*

TIM   I like my little apartment, it's ideal for me. I've lived here for eight years now—how time flies! You remember Martin, don't you?

KATARINA   The one who married—

TIM   No, no, it was Fredrik who married Bettina. She ran off with that little Korean, whatever his name was. No, Martin was in real estate. We lived together for nearly four years, and he gave me this apartment. Then, when we split up . . . He was a really fine person and no mistake. Yes, you met Martin, Katarina darling, I remember distinctly—we were together in Brittany in the summer of 'seventy-one.

KATARINA   Oh, *that* was Martin!

TIM   Now, my sweet, no more to drink. You'll only be sick.

KATARINA   I feel fine.

TIM   All the better, darling. Yes, Martin was a good soul. We were very fond of each other, but as you know, there's no faithfulness—no real faithfulness. If you're gay, you're unfaithful. It's to do with children. I mean the sad fact that we can't have children or even adopt them.

KATARINA   Peter and I are also childless.

TIM   I've always liked children. I think I'd make quite a good mother, don't you?

KATARINA   Yes.

TIM   Martin fell madly in love with a schoolboy. The parents were in an awful state. There was nearly a scandal. I felt very let down, of course, and grieved a lot. Then Martin gave me the apartment to console me. He often came and sat in that chair where you're sitting now. Sometimes he cried. It was awful. We went through a bad patch. That boy was a real devil, just fancy. But I do think the apartment's nice.

KATARINA Very nice.

TIM Do you know what bothers me? The constant noise.

KATARINA It seems fairly quiet to me.

TIM The traffic down on the bridge isn't so bad; it's a continuous roar day and night. No, it's all the boring and hammering. Someone is always putting up bookshelves or hanging pictures or fitting new cupboards or fixing the wiring for an aerial. Then there's a building site round the corner—they start in the middle of the night. I can't understand why workmen have to start in the middle of the night. It must be some form of political aggression, don't you think? *(Laughs and lights a cigarette)* Then the trains keep shunting. And there's all the aircraft. It's as if the whole of space were polluted with noise. Most people don't notice. They're used to it. I never get used to it. I have very keen hearing.

KATARINA You're hypersensitive.

TIM I'm like everyone else. Except that I'm gay, of course.

KATARINA It's a comfort being with you.

TIM How long have we known each other?

KATARINA Fifteen years, Tim!

TIM Heavens above, Katarina.

KATARINA We've known each other for fifteen years and worked together for twelve.

TIM   Are you miserable?

KATARINA   Do I look it?

TIM   You're always so efficient and friendly and self-possessed. Suddenly I got the idea you're awfully miserable. I'm sorry, I didn't mean to embarrass you. You've been working terribly hard of late, maybe you're just tired.

(KATARINA   *shakes her head.*   TIM   *sits looking down at the floor*)

KATARINA   I feel all weepy.

TIM   You have a good cry if you want to. I won't be in the least put out. In fact, I'd be honored. If you want to talk, then talk. If you just want to be quiet, we can listen to music. You know I'm your friend. Or *don't* you know?

KATARINA   Yes. You're my friend, Tim dear.

TIM   Most homosexuals like women. Not because we're particularly feminine but because we're in closer touch with our feelings. Those are Martin's words, not mine, but it may be true all the same.

KATARINA   You see, Tim, it's an unending grief. I've never . . . or perhaps it isn't a grief but a kind of frenzy. I don't know. People like me have never given a thought to the mind, and then when it starts acting up we're in a mess. Do you know what I mean?

TIM   Yes, I do.

KATARINA   First of all, it's just tears. Tears and sobs that get more and more peculiar as they come out. Then the weeping turns to an awful wailing from grief and hopelessness. Then I just howl and howl and howl blindly until I go to pieces.

TIM   *(Gravely)* Perhaps one has to go to pieces now and then. It has happened to me several times in my life. I don't know that I'm particularly upset over my breakdowns. I don't think so. Mostly it has been love. It's like with my over-keen hearing. I'm morbidly dependent on nearness. And where is that to be found? When I say nearness, I mean nearness. The same everlasting wretchedness—first the body's in the way, then the mind. One muddles along on hopes and idle fancies and compromises. Heavens, listen to me theorizing!

KATARINA   I've a present for you.

TIM   A present? For me?

KATARINA   Just a minute. *(Hunts about in her large bag, takes out a small packet)* Here you are.

TIM   Katarina, you darling!

KATARINA   It was really meant for Peter, but he has been naughty, so he can go without.

TIM   *(Opening the packet)* Angel! It's gorgeous! *(Silk scarf)*

KATARINA   I bought it in Milan. I think it will suit you. I've seen you wearing that color sometimes.

TIM   *(At the mirror)* Look! *(Switches on the lamps)* You think it makes me look older?

KATARINA   You don't want to get older.

TIM   The wrinkles don't matter. It's all the ugliness that worries me. The skin that dries up and gets so horribly coarse although I grease it every evening. That deep furrow here by the mouth—I woke up one morning and looked in the mirror and there it was suddenly. I thought I'd had a slight stroke. My neck's not too bad and I've seen worse round the eyes, but my hands are a disaster. I've asked three doctors what on earth I'm to do with my hands. Those brown spots they can remove. But the veins, the flabby skin—it looks ghastly, Katarina. I look at my mouth and hands and can't believe my eyes. I'm a mere child. Or maybe I'm a child no longer? I can't grasp all that about time. Those who have studied the problem say it doesn't exist. It's quite true. I shut my eyes and feel like a ten-year-old—I mean my body too. Then I open them and look in the mirror and there stands a little old man. A childish old man, isn't it odd? *(He puts out the bright lights around the toilet mirror, laughs, and lights a cigarette)* Are you tired of listening? You can have a nap if you like. You know how I love to rattle on, even if no one takes any notice. A childish old man, that's what I am. No, come to that, there's something else.

KATARINA   Something else?

TIM   Something one doesn't speak about.

KATARINA   To me you can say what you like.

TIM   I know, I know.

(KATARINA *waits expectantly.* TIM *smoothes his hair with his right hand, once, several times*)

KATARINA   What is it, Tim?

TIM   One gets like that.

KATARINA   I don't follow.

TIM   One simply gets like that. All I said about nearness is just a dream.

(KATARINA   *is silent and looks at him*)

TIM   Brutality and beastliness. Sometimes I have to go to certain places, you know what I mean. And there I pick up the worst kind. You wouldn't believe your eyes.

(KATARINA   *is silent and looks at him*)

TIM   Big, stupid, brutal, filthy trade. Dangerous bastards.

(KATARINA   *is silent and looks at him*)

TIM   Lust and mad excitement and terror and beastliness. All jumbled up. There you have the childish old man's love life. Not exactly nearness and tenderness.

(KATARINA   *is silent and looks at him*)

TIM   (*Lighting another cigarette*) One day I'll be beaten up and killed, of course. That too has its fascination.

(KATARINA   *is silent and looks at him*)

TIM   I'm governed by forces I cannot master. That's all there is to it. What forces? I don't know. Doctors, lovers, pills, drugs, alcohol, work—nothing helps. They are hidden forces. What are they called? I don't know. Perhaps it's the very act of growing old. Decay. I don't know. Forces I can't control.

(KATARINA   *is silent and looks at him no longer*)

TIM   I bend forward to the mirror and gaze into my face, which is more or less familiar to me, and see that right inside that combination of blood and flesh and nerves and bone are two incompatible . . . I don't know what to call them. Two incompatibles. The dream of nearness, tenderness, fellowship, self-forgetfulness—everything that is alive. And on the other side—violence, filthiness, horror, the threat of death. At times I think it is one and the same urge. I don't know. How can I? My dreams were perhaps too beautiful, and as punishment—life slaps you when you least expect it—as punishment you have your orgasm with your nose so far down in the muck that you nearly choke.

(KATARINA   *has turned away*)

TIM   (*Softly*) Katarina.

KATARINA   Yes?

TIM   Look at me.

(KATARINA   *looks at him in the dusk*)

TIM   Please take my hand.

(KATARINA   *takes his hand*)

TIM   Put it very lightly against your cheek.

(KATARINA   *does so*)

TIM　*(After a pause)* Can you feel my hand?

KATARINA　Yes.

TIM　But can you feel that it's me? *That it's me.*

KATARINA　No. *(Shakes her head)*

TIM　Now you know what I mean.

VII—Conversation with Tomas Isidor Mandelbaum

INTERROGATOR　Can I have your full name, please.

TIM　Tim. T. I. M.

INTERROGATOR　That's your artist's name, your pseudonym or whatever it's called. We want your full civil name.

TIM　My name is Tim. I'm called Tim. Everyone in Europe and America calls me Tim. I don't see why I have to be called something else with you.

INTERROGATOR　*(In a friendly tone)* As far as I can see from the records, your name is Tomas Isidor Mandelbaum.

TIM   If you already know my name, I don't understand why you ask for it.

INTERROGATOR   It is part of our routine. We *must* ask your name so that we don't mix you up with someone else.

TIM   Quite impossible. *(Laughs)*

INTERROGATOR   This is not an interrogation but an informal talk. A confidential, informal conversation.

TIM   In that case, perhaps we can switch off the tape recorder.

INTERROGATOR   *(Still friendly)* Does it bother you?

TIM   If it didn't bother me, I wouldn't ask you to switch it off.

INTERROGATOR   It's off now.

TIM   I am much obliged.

INTERROGATOR   Would you care for a cup of coffee? Or a glass of wine? A cigarette?

TIM   No, thank you.

INTERROGATOR   A little mineral water perhaps? A cup of tea? I'm afraid we haven't a great choice.

TIM   Thank you, but nothing for me.

INTERROGATOR   Then let's get started, Mr. Tim.

TIM   By all means.

INTERROGATOR   I assure you it won't hurt.

TIM   No, I don't suppose it will.

INTERROGATOR   I have asked for this talk as you are a friend of the family.

TIM   I have been Katarina Egerman's closest collaborator for ten—no, twelve—years. For ten years we have worked as partners. The first two years we were employees.

INTERROGATOR   You know Peter Egerman?

TIM   Of course.

INTERROGATOR   How did husband and wife get on together?

TIM   Very well.

INTERROGATOR   In a talk with Peter Egerman's mother I got a different impression.

TIM   Then you've had two conflicting impressions. How madly interesting!

INTERROGATOR   Did you have an affair with Peter Egerman?

TIM   *(After a pause)* No.

INTERROGATOR   You seem doubtful.

TIM   *(Firmly)* At no time did I have an affair with Peter. We never touched each other. At most we shook hands or embraced as good friends do.

INTERROGATOR   I apologize for my bluntness.

TIM   I'm used to it. *(Smiles)*

INTERROGATOR   Did you know the murdered girl?

TIM   Yes.

INTERROGATOR   How well did you know her?

TIM   We were good friends.

INTERROGATOR   How do you come to be closely ac-
quainted with a prostitute?

TIM   I don't know how to take your question, Inspector.
It's either spiteful, insinuating, or naïve. So my answer is that I don't like your question. It is not in
keeping with a "confidential talk." *(Smiles)*

INTERROGATOR   I did not mean to offend you.

TIM   I'll try to believe you.

INTERROGATOR   Do you live alone?

TIM   That's right. I live alone.

INTERROGATOR   This woman supplied you with com-
pany.

TIM   It did happen.

INTERROGATOR   So it was you who brought Peter Egerman and Katarina Krafft together. Or "Ka," as she was
generally known.

TIM   Yes, you could say that.

INTERROGATOR   How did it come about?

TIM   It was one Sunday afternoon last autumn. I was at
the Central Station.

INTERROGATOR   Were you going somewhere?

TIM   There are young boys at the Central Station.
Turks, Yugoslavs, Italians. They like to earn a bit of
money of a Sunday. Suddenly I ran into Peter. He had
just bought some foreign magazines at the international bookstall. We had coffee together. For some
reason I told Peter why I was at the Central Station.

He was rather interested. All at once he said he had
never gone with a prostitute. I recommended Katarina
Krafft, gave him the address, and promised to have a
word with her. That's all there is to it. It's the truth
yet not even half the truth. I was cross with Katarina
Egerman—in principle I've always been cross with
her and liked her at the same time. It amused me to
think of Peter being unfaithful to her with a prostitute. That's not the whole truth either. Weak people
go strange ways. *You* should know that, Inspector. It
torments me that it was I who brought murderer and
victim together, if you'll excuse my putting it so
dramatically. I have a guilty conscience, in fact. I
blame my homosexuality. That's also a half-truth.
This is getting quite interesting, isn't it? The truth is,
of course, that I wanted Peter all to myself. It's ab-
surdly simple. I just didn't realize it. We were to share
a secret. *(Smiles)* Slowly I would win him away from
his wife. I love him, you see. I've loved him for several
years. I saw the awful lovelessness of his marriage and
was obsessed by the thought that he would turn to me,
that at last he would discover me, that he would realize
I loved him deeply. Emotionally, Peter was a dying
man, just as a man can die of hunger or thirst or loss
of blood. I knew I could save him. I felt suddenly that
he was seeking me, that he was trying to get to me. I
don't think I'm mistaken. People of my kind have an
instinct for that sort of thing. What I've told you now
may not be the truth either. Certain wise people consider that blindness is total, that we follow prescribed
patterns, conditioned and raped from birth. Anyway,
it couldn't matter less, all of it. Don't you think? You
haven't got much out of this conversation, have you?
(Smiles, makes a gesture)

INTERROGATOR   I am much obliged for your frankness.

VIII—Peter Egerman Dictates a Memorandum

Flashback in black-and-white

This is what it looks like:

An alpine chain of concrete and glass; it is a winter's afternoon and all the windows are illuminated with a sickly light. At the sides of and behind the office blocks a building is going on: huge cranes, skeleton skyscrapers twisting up toward the darkening sky, half-finished landscapes of iron and steel sticking out savagely. A constant roar can be heard from the motorway. Thousands of people are trying desperately to kill the merciless hours between afternoon coffee and closing time.

(PETER *can be seen high up in one of the tallest office buildings. His corner office, with three windows and furnished with discreet elegance, suggests lasting values and a faith in the future. With the aid of notes, he is dictating a memorandum to a not-so-young and not-so-old secretary with a cheerful and homely appearance*)

PETER ... the meeting was held in accordance with the resolution at the conference—look up the date, will you, it was at the end of last month, wasn't it? New paragraph. Of the two alternatives, that is, either we are liable for the investment costs provided the license fees are raised corresponding to market interest and reasonable amortization, or the opposite party itself is liable for the investment costs, the former is obviously to be preferred. New paragraph. We agreed on an amortization period of seven years. This is admittedly a long time, but as compensation for our service also comprises all repairs, bracket, actually we can gradually replace all worn-out parts, bracket, it is relatively favorable for us. New paragraph.

(PETER *takes off his glasses and gazes at his elegant desk lamp, which, being heavily old-fashioned, contrasts with the room's otherwise light and discreet luxury. He raises his hand and puts it out—puts it on—puts it out—puts it on. Suddenly he seems to have forgotten his secretary, the memorandum, and his important work. The secretary,* MRS. ANDERS, *waits, politely self-effacing but attentive. Her boss behaves differently. She could not say just* how, *but differently without a doubt)*

PETER   As I said, new paragraph. In the choice between a fixed license fee per installation and year or a license fee based on production volume with a guaranteed minimum, the former alternative was preferred. Ob-

viously they're afraid that if we check their bookkeeping, we'll find out the production figures—no, write *when* we check et cetera—and either leak the information or make use of it, in the event of our establishing ourselves in the countries in question at some future date.

(PETER *stops speaking again. He leans back in his chair, then forward. He takes a deep breath)*

PETER The only problem was that an entirely new question was raised. I protested, as I thought it a bit late to bring it up now, but essentially they're right and it will be difficult to reject their demands. New paragraph. They considered, therefore, that in going in for alternative one for calculation of the license fee, this license equipment is paid for in seven years. Even the first extension of the agreement means a total period of seven and a half years; a further extension, ten years. Since at the end of the first extension period the equipment, which moreover remains our property, is already paid off, they consider that after seven years the license fee shall be reduced. New paragraph. In the long run, of course, they are right. It means, however, that even now we must tell them what the equipment costs. Since, when estimating the two alternatives, we have rightly guessed that they would prefer alternative one, we have calculated the costs on the high side. This means that, if after seven years these costs are to be deducted from the license fees, we will obtain lower proceeds than we reckoned with. New paragraph. I promised to let them know before the twenty-second instant. As I am not authorized to discuss our real costs, I suggest that the management should make up its mind at the beginning of next week.

Please take copies for the entire management, for the central archives, for yourself, for me, and for the main file. That's all, Mrs. Anders.

MRS. ANDERS   Would you like some coffee, Mr. Egerman?

PETER   No, thank you.

MRS. ANDERS   May I go at five o'clock? I've a dentist appointment.

PETER   Of course.

MRS. ANDERS   Are you all right?

PETER   I'm fine, thanks.

MRS. ANDERS   Your mother phoned. She wanted to get in touch with you. I said you were in conference.

PETER   Splendid.

MRS. ANDERS   She wanted to remind you that you were to go and see her.

PETER   Thanks.

MRS. ANDERS   The list of repairs to the house is in the file in the top right-hand drawer. Mr. Faber was to phone tomorrow for a decision.

PETER   Thanks. I'll call him.

IX—Peter Egerman Writes to Professor Jensen

(The letter was never sent. Color)

I dreamed that I lay in a deep sleep and that colorful and strongly scented dreams followed one on top of the other with no connection. Easy now, I know just how you are reacting! I'm not going to tell you my dreams; they're boring and private for the most part. I myself always skip any account of dreams in what I happen to be reading, usually because the writer somehow gets my back up by having made it far too easy for himself. Anyone can concoct a lot of drivel in the hope of being supported by experts and idiots. So what I'm going to describe now isn't a dream in the ordinary sense, though what I experienced did happen at night under the influence of sleeping pills and alcohol. If I say that it all seemed much more real and much more horrible than the gray reality of my waking hours, then that is just a platitude. You can chuck it all in the wastebasket—I'm writing not to be entertaining but because I can't help it. To attract other people's attention in serious matters is usually risky. Probably the best thing to do is to go out on to the beach and scream yourself hoarse until the worry over swollen vocal cords overcomes the dread of the closed space. Not only dread, come to that, it's untrue—I have to keep correcting myself because I lack words—always cheated, always led astray. No, not only dread. There was the inexplicable light that came and went—the affinity with my wife, if it was my wife or someone else—the four tones—the timelessness, the peculiar absence of need. Strangest of all . . . No, I'll try to take everything in proper order, if that's possible—my experience hardly has a beginning and still less an end.

First of all I must confess that I witnessed your meeting with Katarina. I was hidden in the hall. I could see and watch you as if you had been actors on a lighted stage. I didn't feel any hatred or contempt. I like you, in spite of the ridiculous way your hair is cut, your arched chest, and your tight-fitting jeans—haven't you noticed that all that is out of fashion? Sometimes, too, I think you smell too much of after-shave and deodorants or whatever it is you use to increase your indisputable sex appeal. I don't reproach you for trying to talk Katarina into a little dalliance. Why shouldn't you want to make love to her? She radiates physical vitality and ambiguous promises. I understand you and I was seized by hilarity at your clumsiness. With Katarina there's a . . . forgive the expression, I don't think you know what I mean . . . with Katarina there's a purity which opens or closes. You made her close up. I'm sorry to be critical, my dear Mogens. I'm sure you're a kind-hearted man and good at your job. I know you take me seriously—I mean what you call my "obsessions." When we had our talk, you tried to listen although you were rushed and a trifle bored. I understand you. All these kinks of the mind that you have to cope with day in and day out, week after week, what a goddamn profession—excuse the term. You were kind enough to confide to me that you lived for your curiosity. You sounded sincere, but I think you were lying. Some other time perhaps I'll tell you why I'm so convinced you were lying, but in a nutshell I think your emptiness and ennui are at least as painful as my obsessions. Is it not so that your hand between the legs of some willing or attractive patient is your only relief from the accelerating misery of being fifty-eight years old? Maybe I'm wrong. Let's discuss the matter another time, eh? I'm now going to tell you—whether it interests you or not—about *the closed space,* but also about the sudden light and the three or four tones. You see, Mogens, I stretch out my hand from my naked, stupid reality, which seems to me so hazy and fluid, and try for a moment—well, maybe a moment is saying too much—anyway, try in awkward words to grasp the clear, sharply outlined reality that struck me the night between Tuesday the twelfth of February and Wednesday the thirteenth of February at three o'clock in the morning.

I dreamed I was asleep, I dreamed that I was dreaming. As I think I've already pointed out, it was all very sensual —I mean in a wider sense, not merely erotic. But in some way there was a distinct connection between the lower part of my body and the nice, strong scent of a woman's moistness, sweat, saliva, the fresh smell of thick hair. With my eyes shut I moved over a wide, shimmering surface and everything was very still. My satisfaction was complete and I felt a comic need of telling a funny story but I lacked the power of speech, something that didn't bother me in the least. On the contrary, I felt that the floating was very much a part of my dumbness and that my brain, my day-consciousness or whatever the hell it's called, was intensely concentrated in my hands, or rather fingertips. On every finger I had a little eye, which, with blinking delight, registered all this gleaming whiteness and the floating itself. It was good like that. It could remain like that. Somewhere far off, far, far off, I could hear laughter and a voice which stated in a matter-of-fact way that liquor and sleeping pills in the right combination were the world's best medicine. During our talk you told me that I didn't believe in the existence of the soul. You implied that my materialism was impenetrable and that "people of my kind" are incapable of grasping a spiritual or let us say extrasensory process. You're quite right. What I am trying to put into clumsy and unfamiliar words is an absolute tangibility, a reality more real than anything I have experienced before or since. I remember quite distinctly that I connected my state with some form of death—I'm so afraid of death—some form of death, which, without complication or cramp, might just as well be my first and complete experience of life—real life. If I were a believer, if I had the very slightest conception of God or of sacred things, I might say that the eyes on my fingers beheld God and that God was undoubtedly of female sex and that the knowledge afforded me a deep and lasting satisfaction. I thought—or rather I didn't think at all, it floated like a multicolored ribbon through my lips: *If you are Death, then welcome, my Death; if you are Life, the life force itself, then welcome, my Life.*

That is the beginning of my "vision" of a timeless and partly amusing, partly horrible experience in the closed space. I shall go on writing to the gruesome end—I can't think of any other word, although it was such a split feeling, but "gruesome" pretty well describes it. I shall go on even if you are already bored and have thrown my screed into the wastebasket. I write, I plead, I call, shout, bellow—can you hear me, or does something closer at hand occupy your thoughts, dear Mogens? If so, it would be only natural. Leave my letter. Put it aside or throw it away. I'm writing for my own sake, not for the sake of God or anyone else. Not even Katarina, although she plays such an important part in what is now about to happen.

(How the hell is this to be done? the reader thinks. Where do we put the camera, what does the background look like, is it a window, can the letter be seen, what sort of paper is it written on? Does he talk the whole time? Is this a boring monologue or will there perhaps be cut-in shots of faces, bodies, twilight, or a stretch of water? It says in the text that he has eyes on his fingers. Are we to order enamel eyes from an

optician and then stick them on to the actor's fingertips? Is it worthwhile at all trying to show a state which is so private that it is almost pornographic? Production schedule, timetable: What's it to be, before lunch and after, until it's time for afternoon coffee? Tests have to be made, of course—or do they? Isn't the whole thing so peculiar that it really ought to be postponed—shelved? I don't know. I'm jotting down words that are to represent pictures that I glimpse. There are no practical solutions—perhaps they will become apparent, perhaps not. I don't know. We can show burning skyscrapers or gorillas; it costs money and effort, but it can be done. But how are we to show a mental process? When was the game up and when did we lose faith in the pictures? When did fear come flowing along like thick porridge, stifling our desire to make dreams come true without any peculiar tricks or smeared-over objectives? And why do the dreams hide, why do they not let themselves be materialized by a machinery ideally suited to capturing the most delicate movements in thought and feeling? Is cinematography—magic, improbable—abolished for good and all, living a humiliated, shadowy existence among film's semiprofessional hippies?)

I am in a closed room with no windows or doors but also with no ceiling or walls, possibly confined in a sphere or an ellipse—I don't know exactly, I could never bring myself to examine the room's contours. The light was gray, fluid, and undefined, rather like a winter's morning just before sunrise. I dreamed that I woke out of a deep sleep. I was lying on the floor, which was as soft as a thick carpet. I felt pleasantly warm and content. A few meters away lay Katarina (or someone representing Katarina), still asleep, unmoving. We were both naked. I knew at once that it was all a dream. I said to myself that this was a dream, much more real than my other reality, it's true, but a dream all the same. I told myself in a loud voice not to be afraid. The only danger is to get

frightened, to be seized by panic, to try to get out, to
begin to cry or scream or to hammer on the walls. I
decided to keep calm. Katarina (if it was Katarina) woke
up slowly. I tried to speak to her but couldn't reach her,
she ignored my presence. I stretched out my arm and
drew her close to me. She was soft and indifferent in an
exciting way and I wanted us to make love but she
avoided me, I could never thrust into her. She looked at
me with half-closed eyes and smiled, moistening her lips
with the tip of her tongue. I hit her and she began to
laugh, but quite silently. I was seized by an insane fury
and drew away so as not to kill her. I was nearly choking
with rage and terror. I was to be calm, not afraid; self-
possessed, not unpredictable. It had all gone wrong. I
could hear Katarina speaking to me but didn't understand what she said. She was in a frenzy. Her face was
quite close to mine and she was shouting words I didn't
understand. I hit her and knocked her over, but she got
up at once and attacked me. We wrestled and fought,
trying to kill each other. At last we were kneeling, facing
one another. (Was it really Katarina? I'm not sure. She
did not have Katarina's eyes or voice, but I recognized
the body, the hair, the forehead.) We were sprawled
against each other, panting with fury and exhaustion.
We tried to talk, but could only speak gibberish, distorted words with no meaning. Everything was gray and
degrading and senseless, but the outlines were sharper
than in reality. The rest of the dream I've forgotten.
That's to say I can recall fragments—short, blurry scenes
that meant something quite different. For instance, there
was what seemed like a reflection of other people—faces
that observed us with excitement and ruthless interest,
pallid, scornful faces with no pity. There was also a
moment of tenderness, of complete silence. It's hard to
describe that particular moment. The air changed,
becoming soft and easy to breathe. The grayness was

dispersed and replaced by a gentle, subdued light like friendly hands stroking our bruised bodies. At the same time, I heard distant music, or maybe it was a song, I'm not sure. It was four simple notes in some major key, soothing and healing. We reached out for one another (perhaps it was Katarina, perhaps it was Katarina after all), we touched one another's wounds, we kissed, I began to cry bitterly. We met in a sudden intimacy without reserve. Then it happened—ghastly, unbelievable, irrevocable. All at once Katarina was dead and I knew that I had killed her in some cruel and painful way. I began to scream with terror and woke up. She was lying prostrate over a table with her legs wide apart and naked from the waist down. The face resting against the gleaming tabletop was swollen, bloodstained, and disfigured. There was no turning back, no mercy. I had killed Katarina without knowing it, without wanting to. I woke up once more and was lying in my bed. The heavy traffic had begun down on the motorway. Everything was as usual. Katarina was asleep at my side, breathing calmly.

Can you help me? Is there any help at all? Can I go on living? Am I in fact alive or was the dream, in the shape it took, my one brief moment of life, of conquered and experienced reality? The mirror is smashed, but what do the splinters reflect?

X—Scene

Flashback in black-and-white

(ARTHUR BRENNER *realizes at once that the situation is serious, that it is not one of the usual rows.* KATARINA'S *face is ravaged, she has been crying, and she seems frightened*)

KATARINA   It was good of you to come. I was at my wits' end to know what to do, you're our only friend. Perhaps you can talk to him. I'm not usually alarmed at his fits, but this time—oh, it's horrible. He's standing out on the roof.

(*It is true.* PETER *is standing on the roof, fifteen floors above the playground with swings and sandpits. He has climbed over the rail of the terrace and onto the very edge of the roof. He is in pajamas and is barefoot. He rocks to and fro in a strangely mechanical way, gazing all the time at the sickening drop*)

ARTHUR   It's quite respectable to jump. But it's inhuman and humiliating to torment your fellow humans in that way.

PETER   What's the time?

ARTHUR   Half-past seven. Someone will catch sight of you soon and call the police. Do you feel cold?

PETER   Yes.

ARTHUR   Can I at least get your fur coat?

PETER   Yes, if you wouldn't mind.

(ARTHUR *goes in and asks* KATARINA *for the coat. They get it from the hall, and when they return* PETER *is stand-*

ing in the living room. He wraps himself in the coat and sits in a deep armchair looking about him. It is a beautiful home, all of it showing evidence of KATARINA's *refinement and good taste. She kneels down and rubs his cold feet with her hands)*

PETER   What affectation, eh?

(He puts his foot on her shoulder and kicks her backward. She falls over and lies there. ARTHUR, *who has been standing with his hands in his overcoat pockets [he has not had time to take off his outdoor things], goes over to the bar. He pours out three glasses of brandy, then goes and bends over* KATARINA)

ARTHUR   Sit here with me.

KATARINA   I'm all right here on the floor.

(She puts the glass down beside her, strokes her long, sturdy legs, and stares darkly at PETER, *who takes a gulp of*

brandy. ARTHUR *puts his drink on a small glass table, pulls off his coat, and sinks into the nearest armchair)*

ARTHUR Martha sends her love.

KATARINA Poor Martha, she was disturbed of course.

ARTHUR Not at all. She had to go to the children's hospital for an early operation.

KATARINA We were with Johan and Marianne for drinks. They wanted to go out for a bite of food, so we went to that new Italian restaurant, you know, the one by the theater. There we ran into Melkers and his lady. They asked us back to their place. By then it was one o'clock. I wasn't keen, but Peter insisted; he said he didn't want to go home.

(She hides her face in her hands, and the thick hair falls forward, exposing her neck. A deep, purple weal can be seen)

ARTHUR What have you done to your neck?

KATARINA Hh!

PETER Her necklace broke.
ARTHUR I see.

PETER I happened to take hold of her necklace and gave it a tug. It broke.

ARTHUR Mind you don't get blood poisoning.

KATARINA Hh!

PETER Katarina wants to leave me, she says. So I say: Leave me by all means, you'd be doing me a great favor. Then she says I can't manage without her. Then I say I manage better without her than with her. Then she says I'm impotent. Then I say it's only with her I'm impotent. And so on.

KATARINA *(Wearily)* The row started with Peter insulting me at the restaurant. At first we laughed, because he was quite amusing, but then he started to mimic me and everyone thought it was embarrassing and I began to cry.

PETER Katarina has an intuitive feeling for the right moment to cry.

KATARINA Now I'll tell you what the row was all about.

PETER The great aria!

ARTHUR Shut up for a moment, Peter. You've given your performance.

KATARINA When we got home this morning Peter was randy and wanted to have sex. I was tired and thought, Okay as long as we get it over quickly. But Peter had something extra in mind, it was to be the big show. I

thought to myself, I can cope with the big show too.
I have before, and as long as I'm stoned I have pa-
tience. So I tossed back a few drinks and undressed
and he started to fuck me before I had got all my
clothes off. I hadn't even washed. I was furious but
said nothing, I just thought, Well, here we go, we just
have to work through the program and then I can
sleep. Then he wanted to fuck me from behind but
couldn't get his prick in, evidently he was too drunk,
and then I started to laugh and he lost his temper and
shouted at me, but I couldn't help laughing, I just
couldn't stop. Then I said I'd suck him off, he usually
likes that, but he took hold of my necklace and twisted
it till I nearly choked. He'd probably have strangled
me if the necklace hadn't broken. Then he went at me
again, he was crazy, striking my face over and over
again, though not very hard. I thought, As long as I
keep calm and don't say anything he'll stop and go to
sleep.

PETER   Katarina told me she had a lover, that's how it all
started. She said that damned Melkers, whom we'd
been eating spaghetti Milanese with, had screwed her
only yesterday, and several times before that.

KATARINA   Peter knew of the affair. I tell him everything. But Peter never dares to tell the truth. He—

PETER   I do tell the truth.

KATARINA   You always lie. You *can't* tell the truth.

PETER   (*Shouting*) I can satisfy you. I know the trick
with Katarina Egerman. Shall I tell you how to
do it?

KATARINA   During the ten years we've been living together you must have given me eight hundred and

thirty-two orgasms. Five hundred and thirteen times I've put on an act and gone into the bathroom and masturbated. At other times I've had a wretched little spasm, it's true. *I'm immensely grateful.* Peter Egerman has made me feel like a woman. You poor sod, Peter. I feel sorry for you. I really feel sorry for you.

PETER   She always goes on like that when she wants to cut me down to size. It's one of Katarina's most refined tricks: the cutting-down ritual.

KATARINA   Am I really supposed to put up with this?

PETER   She'll start talking about her loyalty soon.

KATARINA   My loyalty is an abnormality of my character which has nothing to do with you.

PETER   Now you're hearing the Gramophone record of Katarina's perverted loyalty. Shall we entertain our friend with another of our star turns?

KATARINA   How he yacks away! It's as if he were afraid of silence.

PETER   In silence you hear the truth. That's to say you hear Katarina's truth. *I* don't have any. It is so arranged that Katarina has a contract for life with the objective and genuine world truth. The reason is partly that she is a woman, and as a woman entitled to a special earth and blood insight, partly that she is Katarina, of God elect and created at a propitious moment. I think I must go and lie down for a while. When are we due at Bauer's?

ARTHUR   Ten o'clock. You've time for at least an hour's sleep. And have a nice hot bath. Then you'll feel like a new man.

KATARINA   Shall I help you?

PETER   It's sweet of you, Katarina, but I can manage on my own. Thank you for coming, my dear Arthur, you're a friend indeed. Seeing you and Katarina together I suddenly realize what a handsome couple you would make. As Christ said on the cross: Woman, behold thy son! Behold thy mother!

(He smiles but his face is distorted, his eyes are big and dark, his lips are quivering. KATARINA *has got up. She holds out a hand as if to be reconciled, but he pretends not to see it.* ARTHUR *goes on sitting in his armchair and mumbles something inaudible.* PETER *closes the door.* KATARINA *goes over to the window and looks at the wide view over the city. It is a bleak morning with an overcast sky. There is the muffled roar of traffic from the big bypass and an invisible airplane howls overhead)*

ARTHUR   Maybe you'd better call Mogens. He probably needs a tranquilizer.

KATARINA   He says it's the people around him who are mad, not he.

ARTHUR   That is a very popular theory.

KATARINA   Sometimes I think he's right.

ARTHUR   Peter's conflicts with other people have been microscopic. In all respects he has always been the well-adjusted golden boy.

KATARINA   And behind that handsome face?

ARTHUR   Presumably the same mess as with most of us. *(Stretches and yawns)* I'm not going to shed any tears over Peter Egerman's misunderstood emotional life.

KATARINA   *(Wearily)* No, of course not.

ARTHUR   I miss you.

KATARINA Don't say that.

ARTHUR You know I miss you. *(Sighing)* Oh, well.

KATARINA You speak so strangely about Peter.

ARTHUR I'm fond of him.

KATARINA But you're condescending.

ARTHUR Am I? That has never struck me.

KATARINA A man who stands on a roof in his pajamas and doesn't jump is absurd, isn't he? A man who raves and hits out and bursts into tears is to be despised. Not much—he's a friend after all. But a little. A man who ill-treats a woman in desperation must be out of his mind. He should see a doctor and take a tranquilizer. Isn't that so?

ARTHUR *(Laughing)* Katarina!

KATARINA Actually, you are much more to be pitied than Peter is.

ARTHUR Yes, Peter has you. I haven't.

KATARINA No, I won't scold you.

ARTHUR I play the game, it's very simple. I'm a capable little mechanic. The machines like me.

KATARINA Peter was also a capable mechanic.

ARTHUR That's true. Peter was a skillful mechanic and everyone agreed he would go far. He made just one fatal mistake.

KATARINA Mistake?

ARTHUR He found that the machines are composed of human bodies, nerves, eyes, thoughts, sufferings. And it frightened him. A scared mechanic is a bad mechanic.

KATARINA *(Shaking her head)* It's not so simple.

ARTHUR The grips disgust him.

KATARINA It's worse than that.

ARTHUR You tend to be a little dramatic at times, my dear.

KATARINA There is *something* you must take seriously! Can't you see that? There is something *menacing* going on which we don't speak about because we have no words. What sort of damned idyll is it we are clutching on to tooth and nail, though it is hollow and the decay is oozing through all the holes? Why don't we let all that is black and dangerous come to light? Why do we block up all the exits and pretend it isn't there? Why don't we stop hoping for all kinds of political

wonders, although we hear the roar getting louder and know that the catastrophe is approaching? Why don't we shatter a society that is so dead, so inhuman, so crazy, so humiliating, so poisoned? People try to cry out, but we stuff up their mouths with verbiage. The bombs explode, children are torn to pieces, and the terrorists are punished; but for every terrorist that is killed, ten are standing ready—they are invincible because they are in league with a power that we can't reason with. They are victims like their own victims, just as we are.

ARTHUR   That's all very well, and I respect your convictions—if they *are* convictions and not just the result of a sleepless night.

KATARINA   I don't know.

ARTHUR   Sometime, when the situation is less inflamed, I'll tell you how I view the problem. *(Smiles)* The figures look different, but the result is the same.

KATARINA   *(Indifferently)* The result?

ARTHUR   The "catastrophe" as you call it. Well, I'm going home to have a shave and a bath and go for a long walk with my old dachshund. Good-bye, Katarina my dear. Take care of yourself. May I give you a kiss?

(The curtains in the bedroom are half drawn. PETER *is lying on his bed, undressed, his eyes closed. He is very pale, his mouth is half open.* KATARINA *lies down beside him on the other bed. Long silence)*

KATARINA   Are you asleep?

PETER   No.

KATARINA   How do you feel?

PETER   Fine. I'm fine.

KATARINA   Shall I wake you in an hour?

PETER   There's no point in going to sleep.

KATARINA   I carried on like an hysterical old maid.

(PETER   *doesn't answer*)

KATARINA   What are you thinking of?

PETER   I'm thinking that you are playing the Gramophone record with the refrain: "It was my fault, forgive me, darling." Whoever gets that record started
first is the winner.

KATARINA   But if I really think I did carry on like an
hysterical old maid, am I not to say so?

PETER   No.

KATARINA   What am I to do instead?

PETER   Nothing.

KATARINA   As you wish. *(Violently)* Peter!

PETER   I don't mind your lying here as long as you shut
up.

KATARINA   *(Weeps)* Peter!

PETER   Stop that whimpering.

KATARINA   Yes.

PETER   It won't get you anywhere.

KATARINA   Can't we talk to each other?

PETER   No.

KATARINA   Can't we even try?

PETER   We've tried hundreds of thousands of times. At the next battle we'll use what we've said to each other as a weapon.

KATARINA   Do you remember the beginning of our marriage? The effort we made?

PETER   We had a capital—a capital of love if you like. We squandered it all and got nothing in its place. Do you know why? We accepted the rules of the game without knowing how to play it. And so we were cheated. Do you know what frightens me most of all? Not being able to go to my work, not being able to read my newspaper, not being able to have regular meals. I'm frightened of insomnia, of constipation, of the car breaking down, of being ill, of getting a toothache. I know that every disorder threatens my carefully thought-out safety system.

KATARINA   If it were as you say, you wouldn't drink.

PETER   I drink to give myself courage to put my system out of order.

KATARINA   What do you gain by that?

PETER   I blow myself sky-high.

KATARINA   And what is left?

PETER   A sort of pulp composed of blood and nerves.

KATARINA   Would that be any better?

PETER   I should at any rate be more like the world that surrounds me.

XI—Katarina Egerman Visits Her Mother-in-law

(KATARINA EGERMAN *goes to see her mother-in-law a few days after the catastrophe. It is late in the evening and* KATARINA *finds* CORDELIA *in the large drawing room, which is furnished with somewhat shabby elegance)*

CORDELIA It was good of you to phone.

KATARINA I felt we ought to meet.

(The two women embrace each other on CORDELIA's *initiative. After a moment of strong mutual emotion, reserve and self-control set in)*

CORDELIA May I offer you something?

KATARINA No, thank you.

CORDELIA Perhaps a little later.

KATARINA I can't stay long. I've a client whom I've parked at the theater. I must go out with her afterward.

CORDELIA Of course, Katarina. I quite understand.
(They have seated themselves in a graceful little sofa by the hearth. A fire is crackling and a softly shaded lamp shines on the two women's faces, eyes, mouths, and hands. CORDELIA *has put on an ankle-length peignoir.* KATARINA *is dressed for the late restaurant visit)*

KATARINA Do you mind if I smoke?

CORDELIA Not at all, my dear. Isn't it a strain going out to a restaurant?

KATARINA It's more of a strain being at home.

CORDELIA   Yes, I suppose so.

KATARINA   *(Lighting a cigarette)* We're going to collaborate with a big firm in Los Angeles. It's a marvelous chance to develop. This girl (she actually is a young girl) is here to discuss things and look at our collections.

CORDELIA   Are you up to it?

KATARINA   *(Looking at her)* What do you mean?

CORDELIA   It's different, of course. You're responsible for a lot of people, you have obligations, you have to concentrate the whole time on problems that must be solved. I'm alone here in my big house and don't want to see anyone. I don't even want to go out.

KATARINA   *(Gently)* You should go away for a few months.

CORDELIA   My sister called up and wanted me to come and stay with her in Paris. When her husband retired, they settled down in the country. They've bought a large farm, which they look after themselves.

KATARINA   Do go. The change will do you good.

CORDELIA   Supposing Peter wants me to go and see him?

KATARINA   Have you been?

CORDELIA   *(After a pause)* No. I can't. Not yet.

KATARINA   I went to see him yesterday.

CORDELIA   *(Looks at Katarina in alarm)* Oh.

KATARINA   At the moment he's being given tranquilizers. He doesn't seem quite all there.

CORDELIA   Do you think he suffers?

KATARINA   Professor Jensen says that the shots blot out the torment. He is quite calm.

CORDELIA   If only I could be given a shot too and taken out of this hell. It *is* a hell, Katarina. I'm quite alone here all day long. I put on my coat to go for a walk in the park, but I can't go out. I don't know what to do. I've thought of seeing a doctor, but I only have old Jacobi and he's getting senile.

KATARINA   I can ask Professor Jensen to get in touch with you.

CORDELIA   *(Vaguely)* Yes, that might be a good idea.

KATARINA   I'll phone him tomorrow.

CORDELIA   I'm so lonely, Katarina.

KATARINA   If you like, I'll come and see you every day.

CORDELIA   You've enough of your own worries.

KATARINA   *(Sharply)* So has everyone.

CORDELIA   It's her own fault, you're thinking. You've always been critical of my attitude to Peter.

KATARINA   And you've always been critical of our marriage.

CORDELIA   I'm Peter's mother, Katarina. I'm closer to him than anyone else. I have borne him and brought him up. He is a part of my life. You have no children of your own; you can't understand a mother's feelings. The responsibility, the guilt. *(Pause)* The shame.

KATARINA   *(After a long pause)* I expect you're right. It's beyond me.

CORDELIA   Forgive me. I didn't mean to hurt you.

KATARINA   You didn't. I feel sorry for you.

CORDELIA   I don't think you know what you're saying.

KATARINA   I've been here for half an hour. You've done nothing but talk about your feelings, your difficulties, your guilt, your shame.

CORDELIA   I'm sorry, Katarina. *(Naïvely)* I thought you had come here so that we could have a talk. I thought we could talk about our feelings.

KATARINA   I don't know what I imagined.

CORDELIA   I've thought of you too. Every hour of the day I've thought of you.

KATARINA   I'm also lonely.

CORDELIA   Yes.

(Long pause)

KATARINA   It's no use complaining.

CORDELIA   You don't complain.

KATARINA   I look back on our life, our former reality, in astonishment and think: We were dreaming, we were playing, or what the devil were we doing? This is the real reality. And it's unbearable. I speak, answer, think, get dressed, sleep, and eat—it's a daily compulsion, a hard, peculiar surface. But underneath that surface I'm crying all the time. I cry for my own sake because I can't be as I used to be. What has been can never return—it's broken beyond repair, it's gone, it's like a dream. I cry because of Peter. I've never been able to enter into someone else's feelings or thoughts. Suddenly I think I understand how Peter feels and thinks. I realize he is defenseless and frightened and alone, quite alone. He has turned away, he will never come back however we call to him. But the worst of all, the most horrible of all . . . I can hardly bear to speak about it . . . *(long pause)* is that poor woman. *(Long pause)* I tell myself that maybe she was afraid only for a short moment, that she didn't realize what was happening to her. *(Long pause)* It's no use, it's no use.

XII—Peter and Ka

Flashback in black-and-white

*(The picture shows a room in which sixteen girls strip from
early in the morning until late at night. The performance
takes place in a horseshoe-shaped room brightly lit by multicolored spotlights. The walls are covered with cheap fabrics,
outsized fans, pornographic paintings, inappropriate bamboo
canes, and wilting potted plants. The ceiling consists of a
large window, which is partly boarded over with carelessly
painted bits of wood; the floor is covered with a thick, stained
carpet and puffy, deformed cushions. The latest pop music
blares out of two loudspeakers. The spectators are in small
cells surrounding the stage. Through a tiny window they can
watch what the girls are doing. After one minute and forty
seconds a shutter falls, covering the window. The customer
must then put a coin into a slot machine fixed just under the
peephole in his cell. The shutter then opens for another minute
and forty seconds. The watchers' cells are hermetically sealed
off from the stage and the rooms used by the performers. A fat
man with a peaked cap on his head is sitting by the stage door.
An Alsatian dog is asleep at his feet. In the paved vestibule
one flight below ground level sits an elderly woman with dyed
hair parted in the middle and pale eyes; she has wrapped
herself in a shabby fox coat which was once elegant. Apart
from tickets, the woman sells photographs of the performers,
pornographic magazines and novelties. She chain-smokes.
The girls' quarters behind the closed door are not at all
cramped. A corridor leads from the stage to the common
dressing room, which is brightly lit and overheated by electric
radiators nailed up along the windowless walls. Beyond the
dressing room is a square lounge with battered armchairs and
sofas of different styles. On the floor is a cheap wall-to-wall
carpet which has spent a former life on another floor. In a*

*corner stands a television set which is never switched off.
Newspapers and magazines, overflowing ashtrays, coffee
cups, and plastic-packaged remnants of food litter the two
tables. The concrete ceiling is low, and the strip lighting leaves
no shadows. To right and left in the passage are several doors
to smaller rooms which the girls use when they have a longer
time off or when they practice the other half of their profession. On one side of a short side passage is a washroom and
toilet, and a makeshift office (which actually has space only
for a desk, a shelf, and two chairs). On the other side is the
entrance, which leads to a cellar, some wooden steps, and a
backyard. In the passage, strip lighting and a loudspeaker
churn out the same loud music as on the stage. By the stage
door are two tape recorders and a control panel for the spotlights, but the staff seems to have been done away with in the
interests of economy. The girls' rooms are all exactly alike, as
prison cells. In the middle of the carpeted floor stands a
comparatively large bed. By one wall a narrow bureau or
cupboard, by the other a washstand and a bidet.
    The sixteen girls are of varying ages and professional expe-
rience. They are in good shape despite the strenuous work.
Some of them are even pretty.
    The time is about three o'clock in the morning. One or two
customers are at the small bar out in the paved vestibule. They
are served by a fat girl in a topless dress and with fussy,
housewifely movements.*   PETER   *is standing in a corner
with his hands deep in the pockets of his thick winter overcoat.
He has snow in his dark hair, and his forehead is damp. The*
DOORKEEPER   *with the sleepy Alsatian dog goes through the
narrow passage outside the cells and opens the doors. The
loudspeakers boom out, and the patrons at the bar are rather
noisy. A few spectators are lounging about the corridor, shadowy in the bright colored light. The door to the street opens,
and snow whirls in, followed by an icy draft. The bar closes
and the guests depart. The waitress puts on a thick cardigan
which she has hidden behind the counter. Car engines start up,*

spotlights sweep over the colored windows, leather soles scrape against the stone floor, someone coughs. PETER *is left alone. He waits. The* DOORKEEPER *comes back with his dog)*

DOORKEEPER   She is prepared to stay until six o'clock.

PETER   Thank you.

DOORKEEPER   It's forbidden, by rights.

PETER   I know.

DOORKEEPER   Fire insurance.

PETER   Yes. Thanks a lot.

(He presses a banknote into the DOORKEEPER*'s hand)*

DOORKEEPER   Don't forget you must be out of here by six o'clock. The police sometimes drop in, especially in the mornings. Cops on night shift who want a blow through and a cup of coffee. It's called "routine control" in the police report.

*(*PETER *nods, stubs out his cigarette in an over-full ashtray. The* DOORKEEPER *opens the door and he is standing in the long corridor behind the stage. In the dressing room a young woman is sitting in the glaring light. She is naked except for a necklace of ornate gilded metal discs and a pair of cheap earrings. Her hair is combed back and swept up into a careless bun on the top of her head; on one foot she has a high-heeled shoe. She is busy taking off her makeup. The large face with its prominent features and wide mouth gives an impression of weight. The heated air smells of dust, cheap scent, sweat, and cigarette smoke)*

KA   Come in, I'll soon be ready.

*(*PETER *steps into the dressing room. He sits down on a chair beside* KA*)*

KA   Would you like some wine?

(PETER   nods and she pours some out. He drains the glass and holds it. He is of two minds)

PETER   I'd rather you were made up.

KA   Just as you like.

(She wipes off the grease and obediently begins to put on new makeup)

PETER   If it's not too much trouble.

KA   Not at all. As long as I don't have to put on the eyelashes.

PETER   Of course not.

(KA   and   PETER   sit in silence for some time. She serves him another glass of wine, which he gulps down)

KA   The air in here is very bad, isn't it?

PETER   Yes, I suppose it is.

KA   They forgot the ventilation when they built these premises. We've no windows either, so when we want to air the place we have to open the door to the cellar, but the worst of that is, we get such peculiar guests in that way. Won't you take your coat off?

PETER   Hm? Oh yes.

(He does so. Goes around the rectangular dressing table with its lamps and mirrors; it is littered with all the thousand things that sixteen girls can be thought to bring with them and live with during most hours of the day and night. The DOORKEEPER *appears at the end of the corridor. He shuts off the tape recorders and loudspeakers, puts out the lights on the stage (the door to which is open), calls to his dog, wraps himself in his overcoat, pulls a fur cap right down over his head, and goes out through the door by the cellar. The silence from the switched-off loudspeakers is intense)*

KA   Did you like my number?

PETER   Not particularly.

(He stands in front of her on the other side of the table and watches her as she rouges her cheeks, pretending to be occupied)

PETER   Have you worked here long?

KA   Three years. I came here when it was nice and new.

PETER   Does it pay?

KA   I can't complain.

PETER   Have you any more wine?

KA   The bottles are over there on the shelf by the fridge.

(He sits down at the other end of the room, shaded from the glaring light. He pours himself some wine and lights a cigarette)

PETER   *Prosit.*

KA   *Prosit.*

(KA goes out into the passage, after finding her other shoe. She sits down on the toilet and has a long, enjoyable pee, her back hunched and her thighs pressed together. Then she wipes herself carefully with toilet paper. When she flushes, a mighty roar is heard in the rusty pipes)

KA   You're a bit odd somehow.

PETER   In what way?

KA   There's something odd about you.

PETER   Oh?

KA   Have you done something?

PETER   *(A quick smile)* I don't think so.

KA   One of the other girls wanted to stay as protection. I told her it wasn't necessary. Maybe I was stupid.

PETER   Don't worry.

KA   There's something.

PETER   There's *something*.

KA   Are you afraid in some way?

PETER   Judge of character.

KA   Are you being sarcastic?

PETER   I'm nearly always sarcastic. It's a kind of deformity.

KA It's not very comfortable here. Let's go into one of the other rooms.

(PETER *doesn't answer, merely nods.* KA *gets a key from a cupboard and unlocks a door on the right of the passage*)

PETER Is this your room?

KA I receive clients in here.

PETER It's terribly hot. Can't we open a window?

KA There aren't any windows.

(PETER *pulls aside a curtain, which reveals a blank wall*)

PETER I can't stay here.

KA We can use the stage if you like. It's much bigger and quite nice. Come.

(KA *stops by the little control panel to the left of the entrance, switches on the multicolored lighting, adjusts some levers to soften it, starts the tape recorder, and turns down the volume*)

PETER What's your name?

KA Ka.

PETER It must be short for something.

KA My name's Katarina really.

PETER Then you have the same name as my wife.

KA Well, fancy that. You were going to say something?

PETER You misunderstood me just now. I thought your number was feeble and rather boring. On the other hand, I think that you yourself are attractive.

KA *(Laughing)* Attractive.

PETER Sit over there on the other side, so that I can look at you.

(She gets up obediently and rather clumsily, goes over to the other side of the stage, and sits down on a low chair covered with a stained piece of velvet that matches the curtains on the walls. The tape recorder is playing, the colored cones of light from the spotlights intersect in the hot dusty air)

KA *(With a touch of mockery)* Like this?

PETER It's better if you stand up.

*(*KA *obeys with a set, averted face. She stands leaning against the wall, her hand resting on her hip. She sips at her wine)*

KA *(Same tone of voice)* Is that right?

PETER Look at me.

KA *(Looking at him)* Well?

PETER Don't other men ask you to do much more unpleasant things?

KA This is worse.

*(*PETER *sits leaning back in the same position as before. He has raised his right hand and is holding two fingers lightly pressed to his mouth. The music goes on and on, but softly)*

KA I knew there was something odd about you.

PETER All roads are closed.

(He gets up rather tipsily—almost a whole bottle of wine— shakes his head, and smiles to himself. Then he leaves her standing in the dim, dusty light, leaves her, goes in search of his overcoat and puts it on, looks around for his gloves)

KA   Are you going?

PETER   All roads are closed. I am not saying it out of self-pity. It's a statement.

KA   Why do you talk in that funny way? Take your coat off at least. We needn't just stand here arguing.

(PETER *shakes his head and brushes her aside. He walks quickly to the cellar door and tries to open it. It is locked from outside*)

KA   I told you we always have to keep that door locked.

(PETER *ignores her and goes straight to the main entrance. That door too is locked and the key has been taken out*)

KA   *(Laughing)* You'll have to stay.

(*He breaks out in a cold sweat, sits down on a chair inside the door, passes his hand several times over his face. He fumbles for a cigarette*)

KA   Would you like me to make you some coffee?

PETER   Yes, please.
(*He gets up, exhausted and feeling sick, and stands there undecided.* KA *takes him by the hand and leads him into the girls' sitting room. She settles him in one of the frayed, grubby armchairs*)

PETER   The light's so glaring. Can't it be put out?

KA   We've complained, but no one takes any notice.

(*She busies herself at the hotplate.* PETER *smokes. The tape recorder goes on playing, but softly*)

PETER   What's the smell?

KA   Smell?

PETER   Yes, there's a nasty smell.

KA   There's always a smell down here. Makeup and cigarette smoke and sweat and dust and scent. When the
loo is blocked up, it stinks of shit. Is there anything
else that smells?

PETER   I don't know. Perhaps it's only my imagination.

KA   I'm afraid I've lost my sense of smell. I don't notice
anything. When I was a child, Mama took me with her
to her parents in Denmark. I can still remember the
scent of the seasons.

PETER   The seasons?

KA   Winter smelled of snow and coal stoves and damp
gloves. In summer it was seaweed and anthills. The
spring smelled of melted snow in the deep ditches and
fresh birch leaves and rain. But autumn was the nicest
of all—

(She breaks off. PETER *is sitting with his eyes closed; he looks to be asleep. She stops clattering with coffee cups and percolator, sits down on a stool, takes off her shoes and the overdone earrings, unclasps the necklace with the gilded metal discs)*

PETER   I'm not asleep.

KA   The coffee's ready.

PETER   Thank you.

(She gives him a china mug and he sips the strong coffee. KA *sits on the low stool, leaning forward with her elbows on her thighs)*

KA   Why don't you take off your coat? It's rather hot in here, isn't it?

PETER   Yes.

(PETER *stands up and puts the mug down on a small table cluttered with illustrated magazines. He begins to take off the*

*heavy winter overcoat but suddenly stops in the middle of a
movement.*   KA   *helps him. After the nap, his face is now
very pale and has an anguished, faraway look)*

PETER   I'm tired.

(KA   *raises her large, dry hand and strokes his face)*

KA   What you need is a nice sleep.

XIII—Concluding Conversation
on a High Level

MOGENS   *(Lighting a cigarette)* Peter Egerman never consulted me for any acute mental disorder—as I think
I've already said. All the same, he might have been
seriously ill without knowing it. What causes a short-
circuit reaction like the one we have just witnessed?
Given the circumstances, can anyone commit a murder or other crime? I don't think so. That's not to say
I'm hopeful for man's future. The general madness
that everyone of us so willingly takes part in (on the
whole without protest) shows that each individual as
such is obviously ill, and neither he, society, nor medical science does anything about it. *(Pause)* Forgive me
for digressing—it's a pet theme of mine and I'm apt to
run on and on. As regards our patient, a dominating
mother and a poor contact with his father have undoubtedly resulted in a latent homosexuality which
Peter Egerman himself has hardly been aware of, but

which of course has had a disturbing effect on his relations with his wife and other women. This condition, plus a fear evolving from aggressiveness toward the dominating mother, has not found a natural outlet in Egerman's social environment, in which any form of emotional outburst is considered almost obscene. In this way the patient has cut himself off at an early stage from his emotional life. Instead of being himself he has *adopted attitudes,* playing the part that upbringing and milieu have assigned to him. A strongly developed sense of duty and a self-discipline instilled and practiced since childhood, combined with social success, have hindered the patient from giving any kind of natural expression to his feelings. Moreover, he has manifestly been tied to his wife, who, like the mother, is a possessive and strong-willed personality. The inexplicable anguish, and the fear of this anguish, were ritualized in a closed social pattern in which a certain consumption of drugs and alcohol are an accepted, even recommendable, escape. I venture to state that nothing would have happened if Egerman had remained in his own environment. The disaster is inevitable from the moment he contacts the prostitute. Suddenly everything is possible and Egerman's stored-up aggressiveness toward his wife and mother finds a vent. The murder may have been triggered by a mere trifle—a word, a gesture, an inflection. The girl is killed in a moment of emotional short-circuit. Presumably in a state of ecstasy Egerman commits the sexual act with the dead girl. The emotional avalanche has begun to move. Only someone you kill can you possess—or rather be completely master of. The patient has broken through the social and emotional barriers and is therefore a potential suicide by the same criterion I put forward just now: Only someone who kills himself possesses himself entirely.

INTERROGATOR   What do you suggest, Professor Jensen?

MOGENS   To avoid another tragedy I suggest that Egerman be placed under strict observation and that every
legal procedure that can disturb or alarm him be postponed, so that we have time to make a conclusive
examination of the patient's mental condition. I am
also anxious to point out that what I have said is based
on fairly vague suppositions with no scientific rele-
vance. I hope that our conversation will be regarded
as off the record and merely informative.

INTERROGATOR   Of course. I am most grateful, Professor
Jensen. I'll send you a transcription of our tape record-
ing without delay.

ABOUT THE AUTHOR

Ingmar Bergman has been one of Europe's leading film and theater directors for thirty years. The first of his films to be known in America was *The Seventh Seal*, which was followed by such great films as *Smiles of a Summer Night, Persona, The Virgin Spring, Through a Glass Darkly, Cries and Whispers, Scenes from a Marriage, Face to Face, The Serpent's Egg,* and most recently, *Autumn Sonata*.

Bergman has received every major American and European film prize and is considered by many to be the world's greatest living film director.